W9-AAZ-281

LAND O LAKES®
COLLECTOR™ SERIES

Grilling

Tangy Grilled Chicken, see page 26

Acknowledgments

LAND O LAKES®
COLLECTOR™ SERIES

Land O'Lakes, Inc.

Lydia Botham, *Test Kitchens/Consumer Affairs Director*
Becky Wahlund, *Managing Food Editor*
Mary Sue Peterson, *Coordinating Food Editor*
Carolyn Patten, *Project Coordinator*

Cy DeCosse Incorporated

Barry Benecke, *Vice President, Creative Services*
Becky Landes, *Senior Art Director*
Melissa Erickson, *Senior Project Manager*
Lori Schneider, *Electronic Production*
Laurie Gilbert, *Senior Publishing Production Manager*

Tony Kubat Photography
Pictured on front cover: Glazed Chicken & Orange Salsa (page 22)

Recipes developed and tested by the Land O'Lakes Test Kitchens.

Reproduction in whole or part without written permission is prohibited.
All rights reserved. ©1995 Land O'Lakes, Inc.

Grilling.
p. cm. (Land O Lakes collector series)
Includes index.
ISBN 0-86573-965-X (hardcover)   ISBN 0-86573-955-2 (softcover)
1. Barbecue cookery.   I. Land O'Lakes, Inc.   II. Series.
TX840.B3G7488 1995
641.5'784--dc20

PRINTED IN USA

Introduction

Grilling

Although most of us use the words barbecuing and grilling interchangeably because of certain similarities between the meaning of the two words, there are actually distinct differences in the way the foods are cooked. Grilling is not always barbecuing, but barbecuing is **always** grilling.

Grilling is what most of us do when we set up our charcoal or gas grill to prepare a recipe. The recipes in this book actually fall more into the grilling category than the barbecuing category. **Barbecuing** occurs in an enclosed unit and is a long, smoky cooking over hardwood embers or charcoal with hardwood chunks added. Barbecued meat is cooked very slowly to create the smoky tender meat we associate with a Southern Barbecue. While "barbecued" meats have a thick, sweet, tomato-based sauce characteristic of the South, it is not essential for an authentic "barbecue."

Grilling foods no longer only means traditional hamburgers or ribs, but has extended to marinated tenderloins, stuffed hamburgers, grilled fish pockets and whole grilled roasts. Nothing is exempt; grilled vegetables and fruits have now become commonplace and we feel comfortable serving them to our families and friends.

Enjoy our twists on traditional favorites as well as our new unique recipes, sure to become your new favorites. Welcome to the world of grilling!

Table of Contents

Tips on Grilling 5

Marinades..6

Poultry...16

Beef, Lamb & Pork 36

Fish & Seafood...56

Ribs..70

Kabobs...76

Burgers & Sandwiches 88

On the Side...102

Index..126

Tips on Grilling

Grills

Many types of grills are available. Many sizes, shapes and price ranges are offered. Determine cooking objectives before deciding on the type to purchase.

- Charcoal grills (large size and portable or tabletop)
- Brazier or open grill
- Round covered kettle
- Rectangular or square cooker with a hinged lid
- Gas or electric grill
- Smokers

Fuel

Charcoal briquettes are most commonly used for grilling. All recipes in this cookbook were tested using charcoal briquettes and a gas grill. Other fuels available include:

- Hardwood charcoal (made directly from whole pieces of wood--no additives or fillers)
- Mesquite
- Wood
- Smoking or flavor chips

Each type of fuel imparts a unique flavor to the cooked food.

To determine the number of charcoal briquettes needed, spread a single layer of charcoal briquettes 1 inch beyond the edge of the food for small cuts of meat. For longer-cooking foods, use additional charcoal briquettes in a pyramid shape to provide proper ventilation. For indirect heating, use the same number of coals as for direct heating. Once pushed to the side, they will layer up to four coals deep.

Ignite briquettes 30 to 40 minutes before you intend to cook. Be sure to open any vents on the grill. Light and preheat gas grills according to the manufacturer's directions, usually about 15 minutes. Be sure to keep the hood up when lighting a gas grill. For indirect grilling on a dual control gas grill, use single control, opposite meat placement.

Direct & Indirect Heating

The **direct** cooking method means to place the food on the grill directly over the coals. It is faster, since more intense heat is provided. Faster-cooking meats or thin pieces of meat, poultry or fish are usually grilled over direct heat.

The **indirect** cooking method means to place the food on the grill to the side opposite the coals. It is a slower cooking method because less heat is provided. This minimizes flare-ups if dripping occurs. It is recommended when sugary sauces, glazes or marinades are applied. It also is used for large pieces of poultry, meat, fish or fatty foods to achieve more even cooking.

Marinades

Add or enhance the flavor of your grilled food by using a marinade before cooking. Try Citrus Marinade for a light, fruity flavor or Lemon Parsley Marinade for a subtle, sophisticated taste. Or choose Coconut Chili Marinade to add a bit of zing to your meal!

Citrus Marinade, see page 8

Citrus Marinade

Serve this spicy citrus marinade over tossed greens or a citrus salad.

Preparation time: 30 minutes

- $1/2$ cup vegetable <u>or</u> olive oil
- $1/3$ cup chopped green onions
- $1/4$ cup chopped fresh mint leaves
- $1/4$ cup lemon juice
- $1/4$ cup lime juice
- $1/4$ cup orange juice
- 1 teaspoon finely chopped seeded jalapeño pepper
- 1 teaspoon grated lemon peel
- 1 teaspoon grated orange peel
- 2 tablespoons honey

In medium bowl stir together all ingredients. Use to marinate 2 pounds meat (chicken, pork or fish). Cook as desired. **YIELD:** 2 cups.

Nutrition Facts (1 tablespoon): Calories 35; Protein 0g; Carbohydrate 2g; Fat 3g; Cholesterol 0mg; Sodium 0mg

Lemon Parsley Marinade

This marinade brings a refreshing, light lemon flavor to chicken.

Preparation time: 10 minutes

1/4 cup chopped fresh parsley

1/2 cup chicken broth

1/2 cup lemon juice

4 slices lemon, halved

1/4 teaspoon pepper

3 tablespoons vegetable oil

In medium bowl stir together all ingredients. Use to marinate 2 pounds chicken. Cook as desired. **YIELD:** 1 1/4 cups.

Nutrition Facts (1 tablespoon): Calories 20; Protein 0g; Carbohydrate 1g; Fat 2g; Cholesterol 0mg; Sodium 20mg

Balsamic Vinegar & Fresh Herb Marinade

Balsamic vinegar is becoming an increasingly popular ingredient for flavoring meats and poultry or as a flavoring agent in dressings and marinades.

Preparation time: 20 minutes

1/2 cup olive <u>or</u> vegetable oil

1/3 cup Balsamic vinegar <u>or</u> red wine vinegar

1/3 cup dry red wine <u>or</u> unsweetened red grape juice

1 tablespoon chopped fresh basil leaves*

1 tablespoon chopped fresh oregano leaves**

2 teaspoons firmly packed brown sugar

1/2 teaspoon coarsely ground pepper

2 teaspoons finely chopped shallot***

In medium bowl stir together all ingredients. Use to marinate 2 pounds meat (chicken, pork, beef or fish). Cook as desired. **YIELD:** 1 1/4 cups.

* 1 teaspoon dried basil leaves can be substituted for 1 tablespoon chopped fresh basil leaves.

** 1 teaspoon dried oregano leaves can be substituted for 1 tablespoon chopped fresh oregano leaves.

*** 2 teaspoons chopped green onion can be substituted for 2 teaspoons finely chopped shallot.

Nutrition Facts (1 tablespoon): Calories 50; Protein 0g; Carbohydrate 1g; Fat 5g; Cholesterol 0mg; Sodium 0mg

Red Wine Marinade

Parsley can be easily chopped by putting the fresh parsley in a glass measure and "chopping" it with a pair of scissors.

Preparation time: 30 minutes

1 cup dry red wine <u>or</u> unsweetened red grape juice

¹/₂ cup olive <u>or</u> vegetable oil

¹/₄ cup chopped onion

¹/₄ cup chopped fresh parsley

2 tablespoons chopped fresh tarragon leaves*

¹/₂ teaspoon coarsely ground pepper

2 teaspoons finely chopped fresh garlic

1 teaspoon grated lemon peel

In medium bowl stir together all ingredients. Use to marinate 2 pounds meat (chicken, pork or beef). Cook as desired. **YIELD:** 2 cups.

* 2 teaspoons dried tarragon leaves can be substituted for 2 tablespoons chopped fresh tarragon leaves.

Nutrition Facts (1 tablespoon): Calories 35; Protein 0g; Carbohydrate 0g; Fat 3g; Cholesterol 0mg; Sodium 0mg

Curry Marinade

This recipe combines 10 spices to make a curry mixture.

Preparation time: 20 minutes • Cooking time: 2 minutes

Curry Mixture*

- 1 1/4 teaspoons ground coriander
- 1 teaspoon ground cumin
- 1/2 teaspoon cinnamon
- 1/2 teaspoon turmeric
- 1/8 teaspoon cardamom
- 1/8 teaspoon ground cloves
- 1/8 teaspoon ginger
- 1/8 teaspoon ground nutmeg
- 1/8 teaspoon pepper
- 1/8 teaspoon ground red pepper

Marinade

- 1/4 cup lemon juice
- 1/4 cup vegetable oil
- 1 tablespoon sugar
- 1 teaspoon paprika
- 1 teaspoon finely chopped fresh garlic

In small skillet stir together all curry mixture ingredients. Cook over medium heat, stirring constantly, 2 minutes. DO NOT BURN. Remove from heat; let cool 5 minutes.

In medium bowl stir together all marinade ingredients and curry mixture. Use to marinate 2 pounds meat (chicken, pork or beef). Cook as desired. **YIELD:** 3/4 cup.

* 4 teaspoons purchased prepared ground curry powder can be substituted for curry mixture. Prepared ground curry powder is available in the spice section of large grocery stores.

Nutrition Facts (1 tablespoon): Calories 50; Protein 0g; Carbohydrate 2g; Fat 5g; Cholesterol 0mg; Sodium 0mg

Spicy Salsa Verde & Juniper Berry Marinade

Juniper berries are a bitter blue blackberry native to America.
They are sold dried and used as a flavoring.

Preparation time: 10 minutes

1 (12-ounce) jar (1¹/2 cups) prepared salsa verde*

¹/3 cup chopped fresh parsley

¹/3 cup dry white wine <u>or</u> chicken broth

1 teaspoon juniper berries, crushed**

¹/4 teaspoon coarsely ground pepper

1 teaspoon grated lemon peel

In medium bowl stir together all ingredients. Use to marinate 2 pounds meat (chicken, pork or beef); reserve marinade. Cook meat as desired.

Meanwhile, in 1-quart saucepan bring reserved marinade to a full boil. Serve with cooked meat. **YIELD:** 2 cups.

* Salsa verde can be found in the Mexican section of large grocery stores.

** Juniper berries can be found in the spice section of large grocery stores.

Nutrition Facts (1 tablespoon): Calories 6; Protein 0g; Carbohydrate 1g; Fat 0g; Cholesterol 0mg; Sodium 70mg

Coconut Chili Marinade

Coconut milk is made from equal parts water and coconut milk which are cooked together and then strained.

Preparation time: 30 minutes

1 cup unsweetened coconut milk*

2 tablespoons firmly packed brown sugar

1 tablespoon chili powder

1/2 teaspoon ground coriander

1/2 teaspoon ground cumin

1/2 teaspoon dried red pepper flakes

2 teaspoons finely chopped fresh garlic

2 teaspoons chopped fresh gingerroot**

1 teaspoon grated lemon peel

2 tablespoons lemon juice

In medium bowl stir together all ingredients. Use to marinate 2 pounds chicken. Cook as desired. **YIELD:** 1 1/4 cups.

* 1 cup cream of coconut can be substituted for 1 cup unsweetened coconut milk.

** 1/2 teaspoon ground ginger can be substituted for 2 teaspoons chopped fresh gingerroot.

TIP: Unsweetened coconut milk can be found in the specialty section of large grocery stores.

Nutrition Facts (1 tablespoon): Calories 30; Protein 0g; Carbohydrate 2g; Fat 3g; Cholesterol 0mg; Sodium 5mg

Poultry

Popular with adults and kids, poultry is a natural choice for grilling. Start with chicken and make elegant Apricot Glazed Chicken Breasts or Grilled Garlic Chicken. Serve East Indian Turkey Drumsticks for a new twist or surprise company with Herbed Hickory-Smoked Cornish Hens.

Herbed Hickory-Smoked Cornish Hens, see page 18

Herbed Hickory-Smoked Cornish Hens

Hickory chips are widely used to add flavor to grilled turkey or ham.

Preparation time: 30 minutes • Grilling time: 1 hour 10 minutes

2¹/₂ cups hickory chips

   6 tablespoons LAND O LAKES®
      Butter, melted
   2 tablespoons dry sherry, if
      desired
   1 tablespoon chopped fresh
      sage leaves*
   1 tablespoon chopped fresh
      rosemary**
   1 (16-ounce) bag frozen small
      whole onions, thawed
   4 Cornish game hens, thawed,
      giblets removed
   2 cloves garlic, cut in half
  16 whole sage leaves***

In medium bowl cover hickory chips with water; soak 30 minutes. <u>Prepare grill</u> placing coals to one side; heat until coals are ash white. Make aluminum foil drip pan; place opposite coals. In medium bowl stir together butter, sherry, 1 tablespoon sage and rosemary; <u>reserve 3 tablespoons</u> mixture for basting game hens. Stir onions into remaining butter mixture; set aside.

Rub skin of game hens with cut garlic; place piece of garlic in cavity of each game hen. Loosen skin over breast of each game hen; place 4 sage leaves under skin. Spoon ¹/₄ onion mixture into each game hen; secure opening with metal skewers. Tie legs together. Place game hens on grill over drip pan. Baste with reserved herb butter. Grill 40 minutes; turn and baste. Continue grilling until fork tender (30 to 40 minutes). **YIELD:** 4 servings.

* 1 teaspoon dried sage leaves can be substituted for 1 tablespoon chopped fresh sage leaves.

** 1 teaspoon dried rosemary can be substituted for 1 tablespoon chopped fresh rosemary.

***1 tablespoon dried sage leaves can be substituted for 16 whole sage leaves.

Nutrition Facts (1 serving): Calories 200; Protein 25g; Carbohydrate 0g; Fat 11g; Cholesterol 85mg; Sodium 115mg

East Indian Turkey Drumsticks

Yogurt, cucumber and mint combine to give the sauce served with the grilled turkey drumsticks its ethnic flair.

Preparation time: 40 minutes • Marinating time: 4 hours • Grilling time: 55 minutes

Marinade

- 2 cups low fat or fat free plain yogurt
- 2 tablespoons grated fresh gingerroot*
- 2 tablespoons lime juice
- 1½ teaspoons finely chopped fresh garlic
- 1½ teaspoons cinnamon
- 1 teaspoon ground allspice
- 1 teaspoon ground coriander
- 1 teaspoon ground cumin
- 1 teaspoon salt
- ¼ teaspoon ground red pepper

- 4 (about ¾ pound each) turkey legs
- 4 (12-inch) squares heavy-duty aluminum foil

Cucumber Sauce

- 1¼ cups low fat or fat free plain yogurt
- ½ cup cubed ¼-inch cucumber
- 1 tablespoon chopped fresh mint leaves**
- 1 teaspoon finely chopped fresh garlic
- ½ teaspoon salt

In medium bowl stir together all marinade ingredients <u>except</u> turkey legs and aluminum foil. Pierce turkey all over with tip of sharp knife. Place turkey in plastic food bag; add marinade. Tightly seal bag. Turn bag several times to coat turkey well. Place in 13x9-inch pan. Refrigerate, turning once or twice, at least 4 hours.

<u>Prepare grill</u> placing coals to one side; heat until coals are ash white. Make aluminum foil drip pan; place opposite coals.

Meanwhile, remove turkey from marinade; <u>reserve marinade</u>. Place each turkey leg on bottom half of square of heavy-duty aluminum foil. Top with <u>3 tablespoons</u> marinade. Fold aluminum foil over to enclose turkey; tightly seal. Place aluminum foil packets on grill over drip pan. Cover; grill, turning often, 30 minutes. Move packets and place directly over coals. Continue grilling, turning often, until turkey is fork tender (25 to 35 minutes).

In medium bowl stir together all sauce ingredients. Serve turkey with sauce. **YIELD:** 4 servings (1½ cups sauce).

* 2 teaspoons ground ginger can be substituted for 2 tablespoons grated fresh gingerroot.

** 1½ teaspoons dried mint leaves can be substituted for 1 tablespoon chopped fresh mint leaves.

Nutrition Facts (1 serving): Calories 350; Protein 52g; Carbohydrate 13g; Fat 8g; Cholesterol 190mg; Sodium 830mg

Turkey On The Grill

Juicy, tender turkey, cooked outdoors, is the center of a perfect summer meal.

Preparation time: 30 minutes • Grilling time: 3 hours

Kettle or Covered Grill: Thaw and prepare 10 to 12-pound turkey for roasting as directed on package; do not stuff. Season cavity with salt and brush skin with melted LAND O LAKES® Butter. Prepare grill placing coals to one side; heat until coals are ash white. Make aluminum foil drip pan; place opposite coals. Place top grilling rack over coals and drip pan. Place prepared turkey on grill over drip pan. Open bottom vents directly under coals. Cover grill, positioning top vent directly over side of grill with turkey. Adjust vent as necessary to keep a consistently hot fire. Add coals to fire as necessary. Grill turkey 11 to 20 minutes per pound, turning halfway through the time and basting with LAND O LAKES® Butter. Turkey is done when thermometer inserted into thigh muscle reaches 180 to 185°F.

Gas Grill: Thaw and prepare 10 to 12-pound turkey for roasting as directed on package; do not stuff. Season cavity with salt and brush skin with melted LAND O LAKES® Butter. If dual control gas grill is used, make aluminum foil drip pan; place over coals on one side of grill, then heat other side 10 to 15 minutes on high. If single control gas grill is used, make aluminum foil drip pan; place over one half of coals to block out direct heat, then heat grill 10 to 15 minutes on high. Reduce heat to medium. Replace top rack; place turkey on rack directly above drip pan. Grill turkey on medium heat 11 to 20 minutes per pound, turning halfway through the time and basting with LAND O LAKES® Butter. Turkey is done when thermometer inserted into thigh muscle reaches 180 to 185°F.

Nutrition Facts (3 ounces cooked turkey): Calories 140; Protein 25g; Carbohydrate 0g; Fat 4g; Cholesterol 65mg; Sodium 60mg

Glazed Chicken & Orange Salsa

This simple orange salsa is also delicious served with fish.

Preparation time: 30 minutes • Chilling time: 1 hour • Grilling time: 10 minutes
(Pictured on cover)

Orange Salsa
- 2 medium (1 cup) seedless oranges, segmented, membrane removed, chopped
- 1 tablespoon sugar
- 2 tablespoons sliced green onion
- 2 tablespoons chopped fresh parsley

Chicken
- 2 (12 ounces each) whole boneless chicken breasts, skinned, halved
- 1/2 teaspoon salt
- 1/8 teaspoon pepper

Glaze
- 3 tablespoons LAND O LAKES® Butter, melted
- 1 cup orange juice
- 1 tablespoon cornstarch

In small bowl stir together all orange salsa ingredients; refrigerate at least 1 hour.

Meanwhile, prepare grill; heat until coals are ash white. Sprinkle chicken breasts with salt and pepper.

In 1-quart saucepan stir together all glaze ingredients. Cook over medium heat, stirring constantly, until mixture thickens and comes to a full boil (5 to 7 minutes). Place chicken on grill; brush with glaze. Grill, turning once and brushing with glaze, until chicken is fork tender (10 to 12 minutes). Serve chicken with orange salsa.
YIELD: 4 servings (3/4 cup salsa).

Nutrition Facts (1 serving): Calories 190; Protein 25g; Carbohydrate 11g; Fat 5g; Cholesterol 70mg; Sodium 350mg

Peanut Chicken

Peanut sauce is an Indonesian favorite generally served with chicken.

Preparation time: 30 minutes • Grilling time: 10 minutes

Peanut Sauce

- 1/2 cup chunky-style peanut butter
- 3 tablespoons lemon juice
- 2 tablespoons honey
- 1 tablespoon soy sauce
- 1 tablespoon chopped fresh cilantro
- 1/2 teaspoon finely chopped fresh garlic
- 1/4 teaspoon hot pepper sauce

Paste

- 2 tablespoons grated orange peel
- 1 tablespoon grated fresh gingerroot
- 1 teaspoon finely chopped fresh garlic
- 2 teaspoons vegetable oil

- 1 1/4 pounds boneless skinless chicken thighs*

Prepare grill; heat until coals are ash white. Meanwhile, in small bowl stir together all peanut sauce ingredients; set aside.

In small bowl stir together orange peel, gingerroot and garlic. Stir in oil until paste forms. Spread paste evenly on both sides of chicken thighs. Place chicken on grill. Grill, turning once, until chicken is fork tender (10 to 12 minutes). Serve with peanut sauce.
YIELD: 5 servings (2/3 cup sauce).

* 1 1/2 pounds chicken thighs (bone-in), skinned, can be substituted for 1 1/4 pounds boneless skinless chicken thighs. Grill, turning once, until chicken is fork tender (about 20 minutes).

Nutrition Facts (1 serving): Calories 380; Protein 29g; Carbohydrate 14g; Fat 24g; Cholesterol 80mg; Sodium 410mg

Grilled Lemonade Drummies

Picnic chicken wings grilled with a savory lemonade marinade.

Preparation time: 10 minutes • Marinating time: 8 hours • Grilling time: 20 minutes

Marinade

- 1/3 cup Worcestershire sauce
- 1 (6-ounce) can frozen lemonade concentrate, thawed
- 1 teaspoon celery salt
- 1 teaspoon seasoned salt
- 1/2 teaspoon coarsely ground pepper
- 1/2 teaspoon finely chopped fresh garlic

Drummies

- 3 pounds chicken wing drumettes*

In large plastic food bag place all marinade ingredients; add chicken drumettes. Tightly seal bag. Turn bag several times to coat chicken well. Place in 13x9-inch pan. Refrigerate 8 hours or overnight.

Prepare grill; heat until coals are ash white. Place chicken on grill; brush with marinade. Grill, basting with marinade and turning occasionally, until chicken is fork tender (20 to 25 minutes). **YIELD:** 8 servings.

Oven Directions: Prepare chicken drumettes as directed above. Heat oven to 400°. Line 15x10x1-inch jelly roll pan with aluminum foil. Place chicken in prepared pan. Bake, basting occasionally and turning after half the time, until chicken is fork tender (40 to 45 minutes).

*Chicken wing drumettes are the drumsticklike portion of the chicken wing.

Nutrition Facts (1 serving): Calories 170; Protein 15g; Carbohydrate 4g; Fat 11g; Cholesterol 45mg; Sodium 180mg

Tangy Grilled Chicken

This tangy sauce, slightly spicy, is excellent on chicken, beef and ribs.

Preparation time: 20 minutes • Cooking time: 1 hour • Grilling time: 40 minutes

Sauce

- 2 tablespoons LAND O LAKES® Butter
- 1/4 cup finely chopped onion
- 2 teaspoons finely chopped fresh garlic
- 1 (14 1/2-ounce) can whole tomatoes, coarsely chopped, reserve juice
- 1/4 cup Worcestershire sauce
- 1/4 cup pineapple juice
- 2 tablespoons firmly packed brown sugar
- 1 teaspoon crushed red pepper flakes
- 2 tablespoons cider vinegar
- 2 tablespoons molasses
- 1/4 teaspoon liquid smoke

Chicken

- 1 (3 to 4-pound) frying chicken, cut into 8 pieces

In 2-quart saucepan melt butter over medium heat. Add onion and garlic; continue cooking until onion is crisply tender (1 to 2 minutes). Add tomatoes and reserved juice. Stir in all remaining sauce ingredients. Reduce heat to low; continue cooking 1 hour. Reserve 1 cup sauce; set aside remaining 1 cup sauce.

Meanwhile, prepare grill placing coals to one side; heat until coals are ash white. Make aluminum foil drip pan; place opposite coals. Place chicken on grill over drip pan. Grill, turning occasionally, 25 minutes. Continue grilling, basting occasionally with reserved 1 cup sauce, until chicken is fork tender (15 to 20 minutes). Serve chicken with remaining 1 cup sauce. **YIELD:** 6 servings (2 cups sauce).

Nutrition Facts (1 serving): Calories 200; Protein 28g; Carbohydrate 4g; Fat 8g; Cholesterol 85mg; Sodium 150mg

Grilled Drumsticks With Zesty Dippers

The dips also taste great with vegetable dippers.

Preparation time: 30 minutes • Cooking time: 1 hour • Grilling time: 13 minutes

Sauce

- 2 tablespoons LAND O LAKES® Butter
- 1/4 cup chopped onion
- 2 teaspoons finely chopped fresh garlic
- 1 (14 1/2-ounce) can tomatoes, coarsely chopped, <u>reserve juice</u>
- 1/4 cup Worcestershire sauce
- 3 tablespoons firmly packed brown sugar
- 2 tablespoons white wine vinegar
- 2 tablespoons molasses
- 1 teaspoon hot pepper sauce
- 1/4 teaspoon liquid smoke

- 24 chicken drumsticks, skin removed

Dip

- 2 (16-ounce) cartons (4 cups) LAND O LAKES® Sour Cream (Regular, Light <u>or</u> No•Fat)

In 2-quart saucepan melt butter; add onion and garlic. Cook over medium heat until onion is crisply tender (1 to 2 minutes). Add tomatoes and reserved juice. Stir in all remaining sauce ingredients except chicken drumsticks. Reduce heat to low; continue cooking 1 hour.

Meanwhile, in medium bowl place <u>1 (16-ounce) carton</u> sour cream. For horseradish dip, stir in 3 tablespoons prepared horseradish and 1/2 teaspoon hot pepper sauce. For mustard dip, in medium bowl place remaining 1 (16-ounce) carton sour cream. Stir in 1/4 cup country-style Dijon mustard, 1/4 teaspoon garlic salt and 2 teaspoons white wine vinegar. Cover; refrigerate until ready to serve.

<u>Prepare grill</u> placing coals to one side; heat until coals are ash white. Make aluminum foil drip pan; place opposite coals. Place chicken on grill over drip pan. Grill, turning occasionally, 7 minutes. Continue grilling, basting occasionally with sauce, until chicken is fork tender (6 to 8 minutes). Serve chicken hot or cold with dips.

YIELD: 12 servings (2 cups sauce; 2 cups each dip).

TIP: 4 pounds chicken wing drummies can be substituted for 24 chicken drumsticks. Serve as an appetizer.

Nutrition Facts (1 serving drumsticks only): Calories 160; Protein 25g; Carbohydrate 2g; Fat 5g; Cholesterol 85mg; Sodium 120mg

Grilled Garlic Chicken

This recipe has only six ingredients and terrific flavor, especially if you like garlic!

Preparation time: 30 minutes • Grilling time: 40 minutes

Sauce
1/4 cup LAND O LAKES® Butter, melted

1/4 teaspoon pepper

3 tablespoons finely chopped fresh garlic

2 tablespoons soy sauce

Chicken
1 (3 to 4-pound) whole frying chicken, cut in half

1/4 cup chopped fresh parsley

Prepare grill placing coals to one side; heat until coals are ash white. Make aluminum foil drip pan; place opposite coals. In small bowl stir together all sauce ingredients.

Place chicken halves on grill over drip pan; baste with sauce. Cover; grill, turning and basting occasionally with sauce, for 40 to 60 minutes or until fork tender. Sprinkle with chopped fresh parsley.

YIELD: 4 servings (1/3 cup sauce).

Nutrition Facts (1 serving): Calories 300; Protein 41g; Carbohydrate 1g; Fat 13g; Cholesterol 135mg; Sodium 280mg

Chicken Breasts Southwestern

*Green chilies and salsa add south-of-the-border flavor
to grilled chicken breasts.*

Preparation time: 15 minutes • Grilling time: 14 minutes

Marinade

- 2/3 cup vegetable oil
- 1/3 cup lime juice
- 2 tablespoons chopped green chilies
- 1 teaspoon finely chopped fresh garlic

Chicken

- 2 (12 ounces each) whole boneless chicken breasts, skinned, halved
- 8 (2x1x1/4-inch) slices LAND O LAKES® Cheddar Cheese

  Salsa

In large plastic food bag place all marinade ingredients; add chicken breasts. Tightly seal bag. Turn bag several times to coat chicken well. Place in 13x9-inch pan. Refrigerate at least 45 minutes.

Meanwhile, prepare grill placing coals to one side; heat until coals are ash white. Make aluminum foil drip pan; place opposite coals. Place chicken on grill over drip pan. Grill chicken, turning once, until fork tender (13 to 15 minutes). Top each chicken breast with 2 slices cheese. Continue grilling until cheese begins to melt (1 to 2 minutes). Serve with salsa. **YIELD:** 4 servings.

Nutrition Facts (1 serving): Calories 280; Protein 30g; Carbohydrate 1g; Fat 17g; Cholesterol 90mg; Sodium 170mg

Chicken Vinaigrette Salad

The tangy mustard dressing would also be delicious on cold beef salads.

Preparation time: 30 minutes • Marinating time: 30 minutes • Grilling time: 10 minutes • Chilling time: 2 hours

Dressing

1/2 cup vegetable oil

2 tablespoons white wine vinegar

1 tablespoon stone ground prepared mustard

1 tablespoon honey

Salad

2 (12 ounces each) whole boneless chicken breasts, skinned, halved

1 pound fresh spinach, washed, trimmed, torn into bite-size pieces

6 to 8 radishes, sliced

4 ounces LAND O LAKES® Swiss Cheese, cut into julienne strips

In jar with tight-fitting lid combine all dressing ingredients; shake well. Place chicken breast halves in large plastic food bag; add 1/4 cup dressing. Tightly seal bag. Turn bag several times to coat chicken well. Place in 13x9-inch pan. Refrigerate at least 30 minutes.

Meanwhile, <u>prepare grill</u>; heat until coals are ash white. Place chicken on grill. Grill, turning once, until chicken is fork tender (10 to 12 minutes). Remove from grill. Cover; refrigerate at least 2 hours or until chilled.

Just before serving, in large bowl toss together spinach, radishes and cheese. Portion onto 4 individual plates. Slice chilled chicken breasts diagonally; place one sliced chicken breast on top of each salad. Serve with dressing. **YIELD:** 4 servings.

Nutrition Facts (1 serving): Calories 460; Protein 38g; Carbohydrate 9g; Fat 30g; Cholesterol 100mg; Sodium 260mg

Apricot Glazed Chicken Breasts

Apricots add a fruity flavor to these barbecued chicken breasts.

Preparation time: 30 minutes • Grilling time: 10 minutes

Sauce

- 1 (17-ounce) can apricot halves in syrup, drained
- 1/4 cup chili sauce
- 2 teaspoons firmly packed brown sugar
- 1 teaspoon prepared horseradish

Chicken

- 1/4 cup apricot preserves
- 1 tablespoon lemon juice
- 4 (12 ounces each) whole boneless chicken breasts, skinned, halved

Prepare grill; heat until coals are ash white.

Meanwhile, in 5-cup blender container combine all sauce ingredients. Blend on high speed until smooth. Pour sauce into 1-quart saucepan. Cook over medium heat, stirring occasionally, until heated through (3 to 5 minutes); keep warm.

In small bowl stir together apricot preserves and lemon juice. Place chicken breasts on grill; brush with apricot preserve mixture. Grill 5 minutes; turn. Brush with apricot preserve mixture; continue grilling until chicken is fork tender (5 to 7 minutes). Serve chicken with sauce. **YIELD:** 8 servings (2 cups sauce).

Nutrition Facts (1 serving): Calories 180; Protein 25g; Carbohydrate 14g; Fat 3g; Cholesterol 65mg; Sodium 180mg

Pineapple-Tarragon Chicken Breasts

*Tarragon and the sweet tang of pineapple complement
each other in this delicious chicken.*

Preparation time: 10 minutes • Grilling time: 25 minutes

Sauce

1 (6-ounce) can frozen
   pineapple juice
   concentrate, thawed

1/4 cup honey

1 teaspoon dried tarragon
   leaves

1/2 teaspoon salt

1/8 teaspoon pepper

Chicken

3 (12 ounces each) whole
   boneless chicken breasts,
   skinned, halved

Prepare grill placing coals to one side; heat until coals are ash white.
Make aluminum foil drip pan; place opposite coals. In 1-quart
saucepan stir together all sauce ingredients. Cook over medium heat,
stirring occasionally, until heated through (3 to 5 minutes).

Place chicken breasts on grill over drip pan. Baste with sauce. Grill,
turning and basting occasionally with sauce, until fork tender (25 to
35 minutes). To serve, cook remaining sauce over medium heat, stirring
occasionally, until heated through (3 to 5 minutes). Serve sauce over
chicken. **YIELD:** 6 servings.

TIP: 1 (6-ounce) can frozen orange juice concentrate, thawed, can be substituted
   for pineapple juice concentrate.

*Nutrition Facts (1 serving): Calories 250; Protein 27g; Carbohydrate 28g; Fat 3g;
Cholesterol 75mg; Sodium 240mg*

Beef, Lamb & Pork

Traditional grilling has always included beef, lamb or pork. Here's your chance to try some new recipe ideas. Your family and friends are sure to appreciate hearty Grilled Beef & Pepper Bundles, unique Mint Pesto Lamb Chops or tangy Pork Roast With Rhubarb Chutney.

Mint Pesto Lamb Chops, see page 38

Mint Pesto Lamb Chops

Pesto is made with fresh mint and walnuts, then served with lamb chops and grilled tomatoes.

Preparation time: 30 minutes • Grilling time: 12 minutes

Pesto
- $1/2$ cup chopped walnuts
- $1/2$ cup chopped fresh mint leaves
- $1/3$ cup olive <u>or</u> vegetable oil
- 2 tablespoons freshly grated Parmesan cheese
- $1/4$ teaspoon coarsely ground pepper
- 1 teaspoon finely chopped fresh garlic

Lamb Chops
- $1/8$ teaspoon salt
- $1/8$ teaspoon coarsely ground pepper
- 2 tablespoons olive <u>or</u> vegetable oil
- 6 (1-inch thick) lamb loin chops
- 3 ripe tomatoes, halved
- 2 tablespoons freshly grated Parmesan cheese

<u>Prepare grill</u>; heat until coals are ash white. In medium bowl stir together all pesto ingredients; set aside.

In small bowl stir together salt, $1/8$ teaspoon pepper and 2 tablespoons oil. Brush lamb chops with oil mixture; place on grill. Grill, basting and turning occasionally, until fork tender (10 to 15 minutes). Spoon about <u>1 tablespoon</u> pesto on each lamb chop. Place tomato halves on grill; spoon about <u>1 teaspoon</u> Parmesan cheese on each tomato half. Continue grilling until heated through (2 to 4 minutes). Serve tomato half alongside each lamb chop; serve with remaining pesto. **YIELD:** 6 servings ($3/4$ cup pesto).

<u>Broiler Directions</u>: Prepare pesto and lamb chops as directed above; place on broiler pan. Broil 3 to 5 inches from heat, turning once, until fork tender (10 to 15 minutes). Spoon <u>1 tablespoon</u> pesto on each lamb chop. Place tomato halves on broiler pan; spoon about <u>1 teaspoon</u> Parmesan cheese on each tomato half. Continue broiling until heated through (2 to 4 minutes). Serve tomato half alongside each lamb chop; serve with remaining pesto.

Nutrition Facts (1 serving): Calories 260; Protein 22g; Carbohydrate 5g; Fat 29g; Cholesterol 70mg; Sodium 170mg

Marinated Herb Veal Roast

Veal has a delicate flavor and fine texture.

Preparation time: 30 minutes • Marinating time: 12 hours • Grilling time: 1 hour 30 minutes

Marinade
- 1/4 cup olive <u>or</u> vegetable oil
- 1 tablespoon sugar
- 1 teaspoon dried basil leaves
- 1 teaspoon dried thyme leaves
- 3/4 teaspoon salt
- 1/4 teaspoon pepper
- 2 tablespoons chopped fresh parsley
- 2 teaspoons finely chopped fresh garlic
- 1 tablespoon white wine vinegar

- 1 (2 to 3-pound) boneless shoulder veal roast

Sauce
- 1/2 cup chopped fresh mushrooms
- 1/2 cup chopped red pepper
- 1 teaspoon grated lemon peel
- 2 tablespoons chopped fresh chives

In large plastic food bag place all marinade ingredients <u>except</u> veal roast; add roast. Tightly seal bag. Turn bag several times to coat roast well. Place in 13x9-inch pan. Refrigerate at least 12 hours or overnight.

<u>Prepare grill</u> placing coals to one side; heat until coals are ash white. Prepare aluminum foil drip pan; place opposite coals. Remove roast from marinade; <u>reserve marinade</u>. Place roast on grill over drip pan; cover grill. Grill, basting with marinade occasionally, until meat thermometer reaches 160°F (Medium) or desired doneness (1 1/2 to 2 hours).

In 1-quart saucepan combine remaining marinade and all sauce ingredients <u>except</u> chives. If desired, drippings from drip pan can be added to sauce ingredients. Cook over medium high heat until sauce comes to a full boil; boil 2 minutes. Stir in chives. Serve over carved roast. **YIELD:** 8 servings (1/2 cup sauce).

Nutrition Facts (1 serving): Calories 180; Protein 16g; Carbohydrate 3g; Fat 11g; Cholesterol 70mg; Sodium 260mg

Pork Roast With Rhubarb Chutney

Fruit chutney is delicious served with roasted pork.

Preparation time: 30 minutes • Grilling time: 1 hour 30 minutes • Cooking time: 1 hour

Roast

1 tablespoon chopped fresh rosemary*

$^1/_2$ teaspoon salt

$^1/_4$ teaspoon coarsely ground pepper

1 ($2^1/_2$-pound) boneless pork loin roast

Chutney

2 cups fresh <u>or</u> frozen red raspberries

2 cups fresh <u>or</u> frozen sliced rhubarb

1 stalk ($^1/_2$ cup) celery, sliced

1 medium ($^1/_2$ cup) onion, chopped

$^1/_2$ cup golden raisins

1 cup honey

$^1/_3$ cup raspberry vinegar <u>or</u> white vinegar

1 tablespoon chopped fresh gingerroot**

$^1/_2$ teaspoon cinnamon

$^1/_4$ teaspoon dry mustard

$^1/_8$ teaspoon ground cloves

<u>Prepare grill</u> placing coals to one side; heat until coals are ash white. Make aluminum foil drip pan; place opposite coals. In small bowl stir together rosemary, salt and pepper. Rub mixture all over surface of pork roast. Place roast on grill over drip pan. Cover; grill, turning once, until meat thermometer reaches 160°F (Medium) or desired doneness ($1^1/_2$ to 2 hours). Slice into $^1/_2$-inch slices.

Meanwhile, in 3-quart saucepan combine all chutney ingredients. Cook over medium heat, stirring occasionally, until chutney comes to a full boil (10 to 12 minutes). Reduce heat to low; continue cooking until chutney thickens (about 1 to $1^1/_2$ hours). Remove from heat. Serve pork slices with chutney. **YIELD:** 10 servings (3 cups chutney).

*1 teaspoon dried rosemary can be substituted for 1 tablespoon chopped fresh rosemary.

** $^3/_4$ teaspoon ground ginger can be substituted for 1 tablespoon chopped fresh gingerroot.

Nutrition Facts (1 serving): Calories 340; Protein 27g; Carbohydrate 39g; Fat 9g; Cholesterol 70mg; Sodium 170mg

Pork Chops With Green Peppercorn Sauce

Peppercorns were sometimes used as currency in Europe during the fifteenth century since they were so rare.

Preparation time: 45 minutes • Grilling time: 8 minutes

Sauce

1 cup sliced fresh mushrooms

$1/3$ cup chopped onion

$1/4$ cup LAND O LAKES® Butter

$1/2$ cup dry white wine or chicken broth

$1/3$ cup chicken broth

$1/4$ cup chopped fresh parsley

1 (8-ounce) carton (1 cup) LAND O LAKES® Sour Cream (Regular, Light or No•Fat)

2 to 4 teaspoons green peppercorns in brine, well drained

2 teaspoons country-style Dijon mustard

Chops

1 tablespoon olive or vegetable oil

6 ($3/4$-inch thick) pork chops Coarsely ground pepper

Prepare grill; heat until coals are ash white.

Meanwhile, in 2-quart saucepan stir together mushrooms, onion and butter. Cook over medium heat, stirring occasionally, until mushrooms and onion are tender (8 to 10 minutes). Stir in white wine and chicken broth. Continue cooking, stirring occasionally, until liquid is reduced to about 2 tablespoons (20 to 30 minutes). Stir in parsley, sour cream, peppercorns and mustard. Continue cooking until heated through (5 to 8 minutes).

Meanwhile, brush $1/4$ teaspoon oil on both sides of each pork chop; sprinkle with pepper. Place chops on grill. Cover; grill, turning once, until desired doneness (8 to 10 minutes). Serve chops with peppercorn sauce. **YIELD**: 6 servings ($1^1/4$ cups sauce).

Nutrition Facts (1 serving): Calories 340; Protein 27g; Carbohydrate 6g; Fat 21g; Cholesterol 100mg; Sodium 240mg

Pork Tenderloin With Bourbon Marinade

Serve this special pork next time you're entertaining.

Preparation time: 30 minutes • Marinating time: 8 hours • Grilling time: 14 minutes

Marinade

- $1/3$ cup Bourbon whiskey
- $1/3$ cup soy sauce
- $1/3$ cup Worcestershire sauce
- 1 medium ($1/2$ cup) onion, chopped
- 2 tablespoons country-style Dijon mustard
- 1 tablespoon honey
- $1/4$ teaspoon coarsely ground pepper
- $1/4$ teaspoon Cajun style herb and spice seasoning blend*

Tenderloin

- 2 pounds pork tenderloin

In large plastic food bag place all marinade ingredients; add pork tenderloin. Tightly seal bag. Turn bag several times to coat tenderloin well. Place in 13x9-inch pan. Refrigerate at least 8 hours.

Prepare grill; heat until coals are ash white. Remove tenderloin from marinade; reserve marinade. Place tenderloin on grill. Cover; grill, turning once, until tenderloin is browned (8 to 10 minutes). Place 15x12-inch piece of aluminum foil on grill. Pour marinade in 13x9-inch pan; add grilled tenderloin. Place pan on top of aluminum foil on grill. Continue cooking, turning once, until tenderloin is cooked to desired doneness and marinade comes to a full boil (6 to 10 minutes). Slice into $1/2$-inch slices; serve with marinade. **YIELD:** 8 servings.

* $1/4$ teaspoon any flavor herb and spice seasoning blend (for meat, seafood or chicken) can be substituted for $1/4$ teaspoon Cajun style herb and spice seasoning blend.

Nutrition Facts (1 serving): Calories 200; Protein 26g; Carbohydrate 6g; Fat 4g; Cholesterol 70mg; Sodium 900mg

Grilled Ham With Apple Chutney

Apple and raisin chutney served over ham steak.

Preparation time: 30 minutes • Cooking time: 1 hour 30 minutes • Grilling time: 6 minutes

Chutney
1/2   lemon, pared, chopped

1/2   teaspoon finely chopped fresh garlic

2   medium (2 1/2 cups) tart apples, cored, chopped

1   cup firmly packed brown sugar

1   cup raisins

1   teaspoon grated fresh gingerroot*

1/2   teaspoon salt

1/8   teaspoon ground red pepper

3/4   cup cider vinegar

Ham
1 1/2   pound (1/2-inch thick) ham steak

In 2-quart saucepan combine all chutney ingredients. Cook over low heat, stirring occasionally, until chutney thickens (1 1/2 to 2 hours).

Prepare grill; heat coals until ash white. Place ham steak on grill. Grill until edges are lightly browned (3 to 4 minutes). Turn ham steak over; spread with 1/4 cup chutney. Continue grilling until heated through (3 to 4 minutes). Serve with additional warm chutney.

YIELD: 6 servings (2 cups chutney).

* 1/4 teaspoon ground ginger can be substituted for 1 teaspoon grated fresh gingerroot.

Nutrition Facts (1 serving): Calories 410; Protein 25g; Carbohydrate 66g; Fat 6g; Cholesterol 60mg; Sodium 1560mg

Sweet & Tangy Family Steak

The marinade enhances both the subtle flavor and the tenderness of this popular cut of meat.

Preparation time: 30 minutes • Marinating time: 6 hours • Grilling time: 13 minutes

Marinade

- $1/2$ cup ketchup
- $1/4$ cup country-style Dijon mustard
- 2 tablespoons firmly packed brown sugar
- $1/2$ teaspoon coarsely ground pepper
- $1/4$ teaspoon salt
- 1 teaspoon finely chopped fresh garlic
- 1 tablespoon cider vinegar

Steak

- $1^1/2$ pound (1-inch thick) beef top round steak

In large plastic food bag place all marinade ingredients. Pierce round steak all over with fork; place steak in plastic food bag. Tightly seal bag. Turn bag several times to coat steak well. Place in 13x9-inch pan. Refrigerate at least 6 hours or overnight.

Prepare grill placing coals to one side; heat until coals are ash white. Make aluminum foil drip pan; place opposite coals. Place steak on grill over drip pan. Grill 8 minutes; turn. Brush with marinade; continue grilling until desired doneness (5 to 8 minutes).

Meanwhile, in 1-quart saucepan cook remaining marinade over medium heat until heated through (2 to 4 minutes). To serve, cut steak, on the diagonal, into thin slices. Serve with hot marinade. **YIELD:** 6 servings.

Nutrition Facts (1 serving): Calories 190; Protein 26g; Carbohydrate 12g; Fat 4g; Cholesterol 65mg; Sodium 530mg

Flank Steak In Fajita Marinade

A spicy marinade makes these beef fajitas especially tasty.

Preparation time: 30 minutes • Marinating time: 4 hours • Grilling time: 10 minutes

Marinade
1/2 cup lime juice

1/2 cup vegetable oil

1/3 cup chopped onion

1/4 cup chopped fresh cilantro

1 teaspoon ground cumin

1 teaspoon grated lime peel

1 teaspoon finely chopped seeded jalapeño pepper

1/4 teaspoon coarsely ground pepper

Fajita
1 1/2 pounds beef flank steak or skirt steak

1 tablespoon vegetable oil

1 green pepper, cut into 2x1/4-inch strips

1 medium onion, cut into 1/4-inch slices

12 (8-inch) flour tortillas, warmed

LAND O LAKES® Sour Cream (Regular, Light or No•Fat)

Guacamole

In large plastic food bag place all marinade ingredients; add flank steak. Tightly seal bag. Turn bag several times to coat steak well. Place in 13x9-inch pan. Refrigerate at least 4 hours or overnight.

Prepare grill; heat until coals are ash white. Remove steak from marinade. Place on grill. Grill, turning once, until steak is cooked to desired doneness (10 to 12 minutes). Slice across grain into 1/4-inch slices.

Meanwhile, in 8-inch skillet place 1 tablespoon oil, green pepper and onion slices. Cook over medium high heat, stirring occasionally, until vegetables are crisply tender (6 to 8 minutes). To serve, place steak slices and vegetables in center of each tortilla; top with sour cream and guacamole. **YIELD:** 6 servings.

Nutrition Facts (1 serving): Calories 560; Protein 31g; Carbohydrate 54g; Fat 25g; Cholesterol 60mg; Sodium 460mg

Cheddar Cheese-Pecan Rolled Flank Steak

Slice into this tender, marinated flank steak and discover a moist, flavorful stuffing.

Preparation time: 30 minutes • Marinating time: 6 hours • Grilling time: 40 minutes

Marinade

- 2 medium (1 cup) onions, chopped
- 2 cups pineapple juice
- 1 teaspoon salt
- 1 teaspoon dried thyme leaves
- $1/2$ teaspoon pepper
- $1/2$ teaspoon dried rosemary, crushed
- 2 tablespoons Worcestershire sauce

$1^1/2$ to 2 pounds beef flank steak

Stuffing

- $1^1/2$ cups fresh bread crumbs
- 6 ounces ($1^1/2$ cups) LAND O LAKES® Cheddar Cheese, shredded
- $1/2$ cup chopped pecans
- $1/4$ cup chopped onion
- $1/4$ cup chopped fresh parsley
- $1/2$ teaspoon finely chopped fresh garlic

In large plastic food bag place all marinade ingredients <u>except</u> flank steak. With mallet, pound steak to $1/4$-inch thickness. Place steak in large plastic food bag; tightly seal bag. Turn bag several times to coat steak well. Place in 13x9-inch baking pan. Refrigerate, turning twice, at least 6 hours or overnight.

<u>Prepare grill</u> placing coals to one side; heat until coals are ash white. Make aluminum foil drip pan; place opposite coals. Remove steak from marinade; <u>reserve marinade</u>.

In medium bowl combine all stuffing ingredients. Place stuffing mixture over entire surface of steak, pressing slightly. Tightly roll up steak, jelly roll fashion. Tie with string to secure filling inside roll. Place steak on grill directly over coals. Grill, turning to brown all sides, 10 minutes. Move steak and place over drip pan. Baste with reserved marinade. Cover; grill until desired doneness (30 to 40 minutes). **YIELD:** 8 servings.

Nutrition Facts (1 serving): Calories 330; Protein 25g; Carbohydrate 12g; Fat 20g; Cholesterol 70mg; Sodium 380mg

Beef Tenderloin In Sesame Marinade

Toasting the sesame seeds gives them a more distinct flavor.

Preparation time: 30 minutes • Marinating time: 6 hours • Grilling time: 12 minutes

Marinade

- $1/2$ cup soy sauce
- $1/3$ cup dry red wine or unsweetened red grape juice
- $1/3$ cup Asian sesame oil or sesame oil
- $1/4$ cup chopped green onions
- 2 tablespoons firmly packed brown sugar
- 1 tablespoon sesame seed, toasted
- 1 tablespoon finely chopped fresh garlic
- 2 teaspoons finely chopped fresh gingerroot*
- $1/4$ teaspoon coarsely ground pepper

Tenderloin

- 2 pounds beef tenderloin

In large plastic food bag place all marinade ingredients; add beef tenderloin. Tightly seal bag. Turn bag several times to coat tenderloin well. Place in 13x9-inch pan. Refrigerate at least 6 hours or overnight.

Prepare grill; heat until coals are ash white. Place tenderloin on grill. Cover; grill, turning once, until desired doneness (12 to 15 minutes). If medium or well doneness is desired, move to indirect heat (not over coals) after 12 minutes for an additional 3 to 6 minutes. Slice into $1/2$-inch slices. **YIELD:** 8 servings.

* $1/2$ teaspoon ground ginger can be substituted for 2 teaspoons finely chopped fresh gingerroot.

TIP: Asian sesame oil can be found in the specialty section of large grocery stores.

Nutrition Facts (1 serving): Calories 210; Protein 24g; Carbohydrate 1g; Fat 11g; Cholesterol 70mg; Sodium 310mg

Grilled Beef & Pepper Bundles

Serve these beef and cheese bundles with warm pita bread.

Preparation time: 30 minutes • Marinating time: 10 minutes • Grilling time: 6 minutes

8 (¹/8-inch) slices deli roast beef
4 LAND O LAKES® Pasteurized Process American Cheese Food Singles, cut in half
32 (2 medium) ¹/4-inch strips red pepper
32 (2 medium) ¹/4-inch strips green pepper
1 (8-ounce) bottle Italian dressing (not low calorie)

Prepare grill; heat until coals are ash white.

Meanwhile, fold each slice roast beef in half lengthwise. At one end of each slice place 1 cheese half (lengthwise with roast beef), 4 strips red pepper and 4 strips green pepper. Roll up; secure with toothpick. Place in 9-inch square pan; pour dressing over bundles. Marinate, turning once, 10 minutes. Drain. Place bundles on grill. Grill, turning once, until cheese begins to melt (6 to 7 minutes). **YIELD:** 4 servings.

Nutrition Facts (1 serving): Calories 280; Protein 23g; Carbohydrate 7g; Fat 18g; Cholesterol 75mg; Sodium 450mg

Grilled Steaks With Garden Tomato Basil Sauce

*A wonderfully flavored fresh tomato sauce tastes good
on steaks or other grilled meats.*

Preparation time: 30 minutes • Marinating time: 20 minutes • Grilling time: 10 minutes

Marinade

- 1/4 cup vegetable oil
- 2 teaspoons dried oregano leaves
- 1/2 teaspoon coarsely ground pepper
- 1/8 teaspoon salt
- 2 tablespoons lemon juice

4 to 6 rib-eye or porterhouse beef steaks

Sauce

- 1/4 cup chopped red onion
- 2 medium (2 cups) ripe tomatoes, cubed 1/2-inch*
- 1 (6-ounce) can tomato paste
- 1 tablespoon chopped fresh basil leaves
- 1/8 teaspoon salt
- 1/8 teaspoon ground red pepper
- 2 tablespoons red wine vinegar
- 1 tablespoon lemon juice
- 1/2 teaspoon finely chopped fresh garlic

Prepare grill; heat until coals are ash white.

Meanwhile, in large plastic food bag place all marinade ingredients except rib-eye steaks; add steaks. Tightly seal bag. Turn bag several times to coat steaks well. Place in 13x9-inch pan; let stand 20 minutes.

Meanwhile, in medium bowl stir together all sauce ingredients. In 5-cup blender container place about 1 cup sauce mixture. Cover; blend on high speed until saucy (30 to 45 seconds). Stir back into sauce mixture. Set aside.

Remove steaks from marinade; reserve marinade. Place steaks on grill. Grill, basting with marinade and turning once, until desired doneness (10 to 15 minutes for medium). Serve sauce over steaks.
YIELD: 6 servings.

* 1 (16-ounce) can plum tomatoes can be substituted for 2 medium (2 cups) ripe tomatoes, cubed 1/2-inch.

Nutrition Facts (1 serving): Calories 330; Protein 33g; Carbohydrate 9g; Fat 18g; Cholesterol 90mg; Sodium 370mg

Fish & Seafood

Grilling always seems to make food taste better and fish and seafood is no exception. The delicate flavors and light textures come alive in recipes like Fish Steaks With Sweet Red Pepper Puree, Grilled Salmon With Tarragon Butter and Spicy Cajun Shrimp.

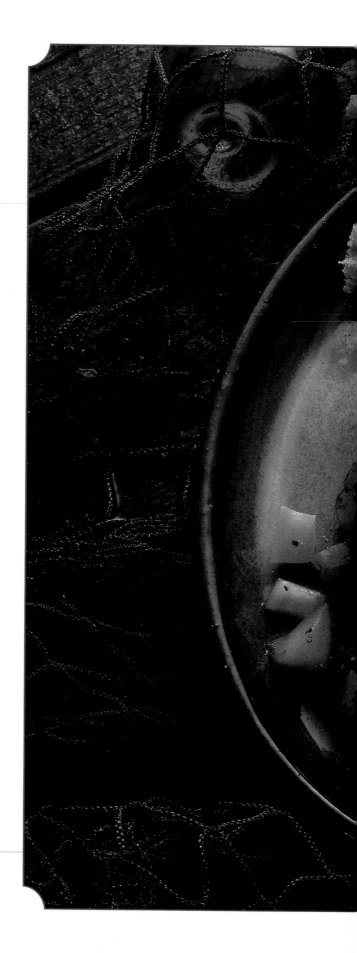

Swordfish With Peach Pepper Salsa, see page 58

Swordfish With Peach Pepper Salsa

This spicy peach salsa would also taste great with grilled chicken or pork.

Preparation time: 30 minutes • Standing time: 1 hour • Grilling time: 8 minutes

Salsa

- 2 large (2 cups) ripe peaches, coarsely chopped (fresh <u>or</u> frozen)
- 1 cup chopped assorted peppers (red, yellow, orange <u>or</u> green)
- 1/4 cup chopped fresh cilantro
- 1/4 cup chopped red onion
- 1/2 teaspoon ground cumin
- 1/2 teaspoon coarsely ground pepper
- 1 teaspoon finely chopped seeded jalapeño pepper
- 1 teaspoon grated lime peel
- 3 tablespoons olive <u>or</u> vegetable oil
- 1 tablespoon lime juice

Swordfish

- 2 pounds swordfish steaks, cut into 6 pieces
- Olive <u>or</u> vegetable oil

In medium bowl stir together all salsa ingredients. Cover; set aside for 1 to 2 hours to blend flavors.

Meanwhile, <u>prepare grill</u>; heat until coals are ash white. Brush swordfish with oil; place on grill. Cover; grill, turning once, until swordfish flakes with a fork (8 to 10 minutes). Serve swordfish with salsa.

YIELD: 6 servings (2 cups salsa).

Nutrition Facts (1 serving): Calories 270; Protein 26g; Carbohydrate 8g; Fat 14g; Cholesterol 50mg; Sodium 115mg

Grilled Garden Vegetables & Sole

Garden vegetables add color and flavor to this grilled fish.

Preparation time: 30 minutes • Grilling time: 10 minutes

1 pound (4 fillets) fresh <u>or</u> frozen sole, thawed, drained

2 medium zucchini, cut into julienne strips

1/2 cup shredded carrot

1/2 small onion, cut into rings

1/4 cup sliced pitted ripe olives

1/2 teaspoon Italian herb seasoning*

1/4 teaspoon garlic salt

2 ounces (1/2 cup) LAND O LAKES® Monterey Jack Cheese, shredded

<u>Prepare grill</u>; heat coals until ash white. Place each sole fillet in center of 18-inch square heavy-duty aluminum foil. Top fillets with zucchini, carrot, onion and olives. Sprinkle with Italian seasoning and garlic salt; sprinkle with cheese. Bring edges of aluminum foil up to center; tightly seal top and sides. Place bundles on grill. Grill until sole flakes with a fork (10 to 14 minutes). **YIELD:** 4 servings.

* 1/8 teaspoon <u>each</u> dried oregano leaves, dried marjoram leaves and dried basil leaves and 1/16 teaspoon rubbed dried sage can be substituted for 1/2 teaspoon Italian herb seasoning.

Nutrition Facts (1 serving): Calories 190; Protein 26g; Carbohydrate 4g; Fat 7g; Cholesterol 65mg; Sodium 360mg

Rainbow Trout With Crunchy Gazpacho

This chunky cold tomato and vegetable sauce, ladled over rainbow trout, presents glorious color and flavor.

Preparation time: 25 minutes • Cooking time: 8 minutes

Gazpacho

- 2 medium (2 cups) ripe tomatoes, cut into $1/2$-inch pieces
- 1 medium (1 cup) cucumber, peeled, cut into $1/2$-inch pieces
- 1 medium (1 cup) red or green pepper, cut into $1/2$-inch pieces
- 1 cup red onion, cut into $1/4$-inch pieces
- $1/4$ cup chopped fresh parsley
- $1/4$ cup olive or vegetable oil
- $1/2$ teaspoon salt
- $1/2$ teaspoon pepper
- 3 tablespoons red wine vinegar
- 1 tablespoon Worcestershire sauce
- $1/4$ teaspoon hot pepper sauce

Trout

- $1/4$ cup LAND O LAKES® Butter
- $1/2$ teaspoon finely chopped fresh garlic
- $1/2$ cup chopped red onion
- $1/4$ cup chopped fresh parsley
- $1/2$ teaspoon salt
- $1/4$ teaspoon pepper
- 6 ($1/2$ to $3/4$-pound) pan-dressed rainbow trout

In medium bowl stir together all gazpacho ingredients. In 5-cup blender container place about <u>2 cups</u> mixture. Cover; blend on high speed until saucy (30 to 45 seconds). Stir back into remaining gazpacho mixture; set aside.

In 10-inch skillet melt butter and garlic until sizzling. In small bowl stir together all remaining trout ingredients <u>except</u> trout. Place about <u>2 tablespoons</u> mixture in cavity of each trout. Place 3 trout in skillet; cook over medium high heat, turning once, until fish flakes with a fork (8 to 10 minutes). Remove to serving platter; keep warm. Repeat with remaining trout. Spoon 1 cup sauce over trout; serve remaining sauce with trout. **YIELD:** 6 servings.

<u>Grilling Directions</u>: Omit butter and garlic. Prepare gazpacho as directed above. <u>Prepare grill</u>; heat until coals are ash white. Prepare trout as directed above. Brush trout with vegetable oil. Grill trout over medium hot coals, turning once, until fish flakes with a fork (14 to 20 minutes). Remove to serving platter. Spoon 1 cup sauce over trout; serve remaining sauce with trout.

Nutrition Facts (1 serving): Calories 420; Protein 34g; Carbohydrate 9g; Fat 27g; Cholesterol 110mg; Sodium 550mg

Fish Steaks With Sweet Red Pepper Puree

Serve these special grilled fish steaks when entertaining friends.

Preparation time: 15 minutes • Marinating time: 2 hours • Broiling time: 5 minutes • Cooking time: 26 minutes • Grilling time: 8 minutes

Marinade

- $1/3$ cup lemon juice
- $1/4$ cup olive <u>or</u> vegetable oil
- 1 tablespoon chopped fresh thyme leaves*
- $1/2$ teaspoon salt

- $1^1/2$ pounds fish steaks (halibut, grouper, amberjack, swordfish, etc.)

Red Pepper Sauce

- 1 red pepper, cut in half, seeded
- $1/3$ cup dry white wine <u>or</u> unsweetened white grape juice
- 2 tablespoons chopped green onions
- $1/2$ cup whipping cream

In small bowl stir together all marinade ingredients. Place fish steaks in 8-inch glass baking dish; pour marinade over fish. Cover with plastic food wrap; refrigerate 2 hours.

Meanwhile, place red pepper halves, cut side down, on broiler pan. Broil 4 to 6 inches from heat until skin blackens (5 to 10 minutes). Wrap in damp paper towels; place in plastic food bag. Let stand 10 minutes.

Peel skins from peppers; discard skin. In 5-cup blender container place peppers. Cover; blend at high until smooth (30 to 45 seconds). Pour into 1-quart saucepan. Stir in white wine and green onions. Cook over medium heat, stirring occasionally, until sauce comes to a full boil (6 to 8 minutes). Reduce heat to low; continue cooking, stirring occasionally, until flavors blend and sauce thickens slightly (12 to 15 minutes). Stir in whipping cream. Continue cooking until sauce is heated through (8 to 10 minutes).

Meanwhile, <u>prepare grill</u>; heat until coals are ash white. Place fish on grill. Cover; grill, turning once, until fish flakes with a fork (8 to 10 minutes). On each serving plate place about <u>3 tablespoons</u> red pepper sauce; top with fish. **YIELD:** 4 servings (1 cup sauce).

* 1 teaspoon dried thyme leaves can be substituted for 1 tablespoon chopped fresh thyme leaves.

Nutrition Facts (1 serving): Calories 290; Protein 29g; Carbohydrate 3g; Fat 16g; Cholesterol 95mg; Sodium 160mg

Grilled Salmon With Tarragon Butter

Tarragon is an aromatic herb with a distinct aniselike flavor.

Preparation time: 30 minutes • Grilling time: 10 minutes

1/2 cup LAND O LAKES®
    Butter, softened
1 tablespoon chopped fresh
    tarragon leaves*
1 teaspoon lemon juice

4 (1-inch thick) salmon steaks

<u>Prepare grill</u> placing coals to one side; heat until coals are ash white. Make aluminum foil drip pan; place opposite coals.

Meanwhile, in small bowl stir together butter, tarragon and lemon juice. Divide butter mixture in half; reserve half. Spread <u>1 teaspoon</u> butter mixture on both sides of each salmon steak. Grill, turning once, until salmon flakes with a fork (10 to 12 minutes). Serve salmon with reserved butter mixture. **YIELD:** 4 servings.

* 1 teaspoon dried tarragon leaves can be substituted for 1 tablespoon chopped fresh tarragon leaves.

Nutrition Facts (1 serving): Calories 340; Protein 19g; Carbohydrate 0g; Fat 29g; Cholesterol 115mg; Sodium 280mg

Grilled Fish Florentine

The term florentine, *meaning "in the style of Florence (Italy)", is often used in reference to dishes that contain spinach.*

Preparation time: 30 minutes • Grilling time: 10 minutes

Stuffing

- 3 tablespoons LAND O LAKES® Butter
- 1/4 cup chopped onion
- 1/2 pound fresh spinach, torn into pieces*
- 4 ounces (1 cup) LAND O LAKES® Cheddar Cheese, shredded
- 3/4 cup dried crumbly style plain stuffing
- 1 (2-ounce) jar diced pimiento, drained
- 1/4 teaspoon salt
- 1/8 teaspoon pepper

Fish

- 1 pound (4 fillets) fresh or frozen sole, thawed, drained

<u>Prepare grill</u>; heat until coals are ash white.

Meanwhile, in 10-inch skillet melt butter; add onion and spinach. Cook over medium heat, stirring occasionally, until tender (4 to 5 minutes); remove from heat. Stir in cheese, stuffing, pimiento, salt and pepper.

Place each sole fillet in center of 18-inch square heavy-duty aluminum foil. Place <u>1/3 cup</u> stuffing on top of each sole fillet. Bring edges of aluminum foil up to center; tightly seal top and sides. Place bundles on grill. Grill until sole flakes with a fork (10 to 14 minutes).
YIELD: 4 servings.

* 1 (10-ounce) package frozen chopped spinach, thawed, drained, can be substituted for 1/2 pound fresh spinach, torn into pieces.

Nutrition Facts (1 serving): Calories 390; Protein 27g; Carbohydrate 12g; Fat 27g; Cholesterol 75mg; Sodium 660mg

Sea Bass With Mango Lime Salsa

This chunky Caribbean-inspired salsa is flavorful
and colorful served over grilled sea bass.

Preparation time: 30 minutes • Standing time: 1 hour • Grilling time: 8 minutes

Salsa

- 1 large (about 2 cups) ripe mango, peeled, cut into $1/2$-inch cubes
- 1 large (1 cup) ripe tomato, seeded, coarsely chopped
- 2 tablespoons chopped fresh chives
- 1 tablespoon chopped fresh mint leaves*
- 2 teaspoons chopped fresh gingerroot**
- 1 teaspoon grated lime peel
- 1 tablespoon lime juice
- 2 teaspoons vegetable oil

Sea Bass

- 2 pounds sea bass steaks <u>or</u> fillets, scales removed
  Vegetable oil

In medium bowl stir together all salsa ingredients. Cover; set aside for 1 to 2 hours to blend flavors.

Meanwhile, <u>prepare grill</u>; heat until coals are ash white. Brush sea bass steaks with oil; place on grill. Cover; grill, turning once, until sea bass flakes with a fork (8 to 10 minutes). Serve sea bass with salsa.

YIELD: 8 servings (2 cups salsa).

---

* 1 teaspoon dried mint leaves can be substituted for 1 tablespoon chopped fresh mint leaves.

** $1/2$ teaspoon ground ginger can be substituted for 2 teaspoons chopped fresh gingerroot.

Nutrition Facts (1 serving): Calories 150; Protein 18g; Carbohydrate 8g; Fat 5g; Cholesterol 40mg; Sodium 70mg

Spicy Cajun Shrimp

A spicy Cajun sauce complements fresh shrimp.

Preparation time: 20 minutes • Grilling time: 6 minutes

Sauce

- 1/4 cup LAND O LAKES® Butter
- 1 teaspoon chopped fresh thyme leaves*
- 1/2 teaspoon pepper
- 1/8 to 1/4 teaspoon ground red pepper
- 2 tablespoons ketchup
- 1 teaspoon Worcestershire sauce
- 1/2 teaspoon finely chopped fresh garlic

Kabobs

- 1 pound (20 to 25) fresh raw shrimp, cleaned, shelled, deveined
- 8 green onions, each cut into 3 (2-inch) pieces
- 2 lemons, each cut into 6 slices, then cut in half

- 12 (6-inch) wooden skewers, soaked in water

Prepare grill; heat until coals are ash white.

Meanwhile, in 1-quart saucepan combine all sauce ingredients. Cook over medium heat, stirring occasionally, until butter is melted (4 to 5 minutes).

To assemble kabobs on each wooden skewer place 1 shrimp, 1 green onion piece, 1 lemon slice, 1 shrimp and 1 green onion piece; brush with sauce. Place kabobs on grill. Grill, brushing with sauce and turning frequently, until shrimp turn pink (6 to 10 minutes). **YIELD:** 4 servings.

* 1/4 teaspoon dried thyme leaves can be substituted for 1 teaspoon chopped fresh thyme leaves.

Nutrition Facts (1 serving): Calories 240; Protein 20g; Carbohydrate 12g; Fat 14g; Cholesterol 160mg; Sodium 340mg

Ribs

Tender and flavorful, ribs are a favorite grilling choice. Make mellow Honey Mustard Glazed Ribs, traditional Sweet & Tangy Barbecue Sauce With Country-Style Ribs or a Western Barbecued Rib Sampler for an outdoor barbecue.

Honey Mustard Glazed Ribs, see page 72

Honey Mustard Glazed Ribs

Use a fresh orange for optimum flavor in the glaze.

Preparation time: 30 minutes • Cooking time: 20 minutes • Grilling time: 1 hour

Glaze

- 1 medium ($^1/_2$ cup) onion, chopped
- 2 tablespoons LAND O LAKES® Butter
- 1 cup honey
- $^1/_3$ cup white wine vinegar
- 1 (8-ounce) jar country-style Dijon mustard
- $^1/_2$ teaspoon salt
- $^1/_2$ teaspoon grated orange peel
- 2 tablespoons orange juice

Ribs

- 4 pounds pork loin <u>or</u> spareribs

In 2-quart saucepan place onion and butter. Cook over medium heat, stirring occasionally, until onion is tender (6 to 8 minutes). Stir in all remaining glaze ingredients. Continue cooking, stirring occasionally, until mixture comes to a full boil (6 to 8 minutes). Turn heat to medium low; continue cooking until sauce thickens slightly and flavors blend (8 to 10 minutes). Remove from heat; <u>reserve $^1/_2$ cup glaze</u>. Set aside remaining glaze.

Meanwhile, <u>prepare grill</u>; heat until coals are ash white. Make aluminum foil drip pan; place opposite coals. Place ribs on grill over drip pan. Cover; grill, turning once, until ribs are browned (40 to 50 minutes). Brush tops of ribs with <u>$^1/_4$ cup</u> reserved glaze; continue grilling for 10 to 15 minutes. Turn ribs; brush with remaining $^1/_4$ cup reserved glaze. Continue grilling until ribs are fork tender (10 to 15 minutes). Serve with remaining glaze. **YIELD:** 6 servings (2 cups glaze).

TIP: Glaze can also be used on chicken, pork or beef.

Nutrition Facts (1 serving): Calories 710; Protein 36g; Carbohydrate 51g; Fat 41g; Cholesterol 155mg; Sodium 800mg

Sweet & Tangy Barbecue Sauce With Country-Style Ribs

Brush this sweet, spicy barbecue sauce on chicken, pork or beef next time you barbecue.

Preparation time: 30 minutes • Cooking time: 1 hour 12 minutes • Grilling time: 20 minutes

Sauce

- 1/3 cup firmly packed brown sugar
- 2 medium (1 cup) onions, chopped
- 1/4 cup LAND O LAKES® Butter
- 1/3 cup apple cider
- 1/3 cup dry red wine <u>or</u> unsweetened red grape juice
- 1/4 cup red wine vinegar
- 2 tablespoons sweet hot mustard
- 2 tablespoons Worcestershire sauce
- 1 (14-ounce) bottle (1 1/2 cups) ketchup
- 1 teaspoon paprika
- 1/2 teaspoon salt
- 1/4 teaspoon coarsely ground pepper
- 1/8 teaspoon ground red pepper
- 2 teaspoons finely chopped fresh garlic
- 1 teaspoon grated fresh gingerroot*

Ribs

- 6 pounds country-style pork ribs
- 6 cups water

In 3-quart saucepan combine all sauce ingredients. Cover; cook over medium heat, stirring occasionally, until sauce comes to a full boil (12 to 15 minutes). Reduce heat to low; uncover. Continue cooking, stirring occasionally, until sauce is thickened and flavors are blended (about 1 hour).

Meanwhile, in Dutch oven combine ribs and water. Cover; cook over medium heat, stirring occasionally, until water comes to a full boil (30 to 40 minutes). Reduce heat to low; continue cooking until ribs are fork tender (30 to 35 minutes). Drain; pat dry.

Meanwhile, <u>prepare grill</u>; heat until coals are ash white. Make aluminum foil drip pan; place opposite coals. Place ribs on grill over drip pan. Brush with sauce. Cover; grill, turning occasionally and brushing with sauce, until fork tender and heated through (20 to 25 minutes). In 3-quart saucepan cook remaining sauce over medium heat until mixture comes to a full boil (4 to 5 minutes); boil 2 minutes. Serve ribs with additional sauce. **YIELD:** 6 servings (2 1/2 cups sauce).

* 1/4 teaspoon ground ginger can be substituted for 1 teaspoon grated fresh gingerroot.

TIP: Sauce can also be used on chicken, pork or beef.

TIP: Ribs are precooked to shorten grilling time and tenderize meat.

Nutrition Facts (1 serving): Calories 570; Protein 47g; Carbohydrate 36g; Fat 26g; Cholesterol 135mg; Sodium 1240mg

Western Barbecued Rib Sample

*Ribs are simmered in beer, then coated with a flavorful,
hot and spicy barbecue sauce.*

Preparation time: 30 minutes • Cooking time: 45 minutes • Grilling time: 12 minutes

Ribs

- ½ cup firmly packed brown sugar
- ¼ cup country-style Dijon mustard
- 2 (12-ounce) cans beer <u>or</u> non-alcoholic beer*
- 1 teaspoon hot pepper sauce
- 3 pounds country-style beef <u>or</u> pork ribs

Barbecue Sauce

- ¼ cup firmly packed brown sugar
- ¼ cup chopped onion
- 1 cup ketchup
- ½ cup Worcestershire sauce
- ¼ cup lemon juice
- ½ teaspoon coarsely ground pepper
- ¼ teaspoon ground red pepper
- ¼ teaspoon salt

In Dutch oven stir together all rib ingredients <u>except</u> ribs; add ribs. Cook over high heat until mixture comes to a full boil (5 to 10 minutes). Cover; reduce heat to low. Continue cooking, turning ribs occasionally, until ribs are fork tender (40 to 50 minutes).

Meanwhile, <u>prepare grill</u>; heat until coals are ash white. In 1-quart saucepan stir together all barbecue sauce ingredients. Place ribs on grill. Brush ribs with barbecue sauce. Grill, brushing with barbecue sauce and turning occasionally, until ribs are fork tender and heated through (12 to 15 minutes). In 1-quart saucepan cook remaining barbecue sauce over medium heat, stirring occasionally, until just comes to a boil (3 to 5 minutes). Serve ribs with additional sauce. **YIELD:** 4 servings.

<u>Broiling Directions</u>: Prepare ribs as directed above. Do not grill. Heat broiler. Line broiler pan with aluminum foil; grease. Place ribs on prepared broiler pan 5 to 7 inches from heat. Brush with barbecue sauce. Broil, brushing with barbecue sauce and turning occasionally, until ribs are done (6 to 8 minutes). Cook remaining barbecue sauce over medium heat, stirring occasionally, until just comes to a boil (3 to 5 minutes). Serve with ribs.

*3 cups apple juice can be substituted for 2 (12-ounce) cans beer.

Nutrition Facts (1 serving): Calories 680; Protein 40g; Carbohydrate 70g; Fat 21g; Cholesterol 115mg; Sodium 1750mg

Kabobs

Easy to create, kabobs make any meal more fun. Try Beef Kabobs With Horseradish Sauce for a dish with some kick! Ask the kids to help with Grilled Fruit Kabobs With Coconut Cream Dip. And serve Swordfish Kabobs when friends come over.

Teriyaki Chicken Kabobs, see page 78

Teriyaki Chicken Kabobs

The brown sugar in this marinade gives these kabobs a light glaze.

Preparation time: 30 minutes • Marinating time: 3 hours • Grilling time: 15 minutes

Marinade

- ⅓ cup lemon juice
- ¼ cup LAND O LAKES® Butter, melted
- ¼ cup soy sauce
- 2 tablespoons firmly packed brown sugar
- ½ teaspoon ground ginger
- ¼ teaspoon pepper
- 3 tablespoons ketchup
- 1 teaspoon finely chopped fresh garlic

Chicken

- 1 pound boneless chicken breast, cut into about 32 (1-inch) pieces

Kabobs

- 8 (1-inch) pineapple chunks
- 8 cherry tomatoes
- 1 small green pepper, cut into 8 (1-inch) pieces
- 1 small zucchini, cut into 8 (1-inch) pieces

- 4 (12-inch) metal skewers

  Hot cooked wild rice

In large plastic food bag combine all marinade ingredients; add chicken pieces. Tightly seal bag. Turn bag several times to coat chicken well. Place in 13x9-inch pan. Refrigerate, turning occasionally, at least 3 hours. Drain; reserve marinade.

Prepare grill placing coals to one side; heat until coals are ash white. Make aluminum foil drip pan; place opposite coals. To assemble kabobs on metal skewers alternately thread chicken, pineapple, tomatoes, green pepper and zucchini. Brush kabobs with marinade. Place kabobs on grill over drip pan. Grill, turning and basting with marinade occasionally, until chicken is fork tender (15 to 20 minutes). Serve with wild rice. **YIELD:** 4 servings.

Nutrition Facts (1 serving without rice): Calories 240; Protein 26g; Carbohydrate 15g; Fat 9g; Cholesterol 80mg; Sodium 720mg

Company's Coming Kabobs

These kabobs can be assembled ahead of time, covered and refrigerated until the party starts!

Preparation time: 30 minutes • Marinating time: 20 minutes • Grilling time: 8 minutes

Chicken

4 (12 ounces each) whole boneless chicken breasts, skinned, cut into 1-inch pieces

1 (20-ounce) can pineapple chunks in heavy syrup, drained, <u>reserve syrup</u>

Marinade

²/₃ cup reserved pineapple syrup

¹/₄ cup honey

¹/₂ teaspoon salt

¹/₄ teaspoon ground ginger

¹/₄ teaspoon pepper

Kabobs

12 cherry tomatoes

2 medium onions, cut into eighths

2 medium green peppers, cut into 2-inch pieces

6 (12-inch) metal skewers

In medium bowl place chicken pieces. Set aside pineapple chunks. In 2-quart saucepan stir together all marinade ingredients. Cook over medium heat, stirring occasionally, until honey is melted (2 to 3 minutes). Pour over chicken; marinate, stirring occasionally, 20 minutes. Drain; <u>reserve marinade</u>.

Meanwhile, <u>prepare grill</u> placing coals to one side; heat until coals are ash white. Make aluminum foil drip pan; place opposite coals. To assemble kabobs on metal skewers alternately thread chicken, tomatoes, onions, green peppers and pineapple chunks. Place kabobs on grill over drip pan. Grill, turning and basting occasionally, until chicken is fork tender (8 to 12 minutes). In 1-quart saucepan cook remaining marinade over medium heat, stirring occasionally, until mixture comes to a full boil (2 to 3 minutes); boil 2 minutes. Just before serving, spoon marinade over kabobs. **YIELD:** 6 servings.

Nutrition Facts (1 serving): Calories 310; Protein 37g; Carbohydrate 32g; Fat 4g; Cholesterol 95mg; Sodium 270mg

Beef Kabobs With Horseradish Sauce

Horseradish has a pungent, spicy flavor that tastes especially delicious with beef.

Preparation time: 30 minutes • Marinating time: 30 minutes • Grilling time: 10 minutes

Kabobs

1 pound beef sirloin, cut into about 32 (1-inch) pieces

1/4 cup Italian dressing

8 small fresh mushrooms

8 cherry tomatoes

1 small green pepper, cut into 8 (1-inch) pieces

1 small onion, cut into 8 wedges

4 (12-inch) metal skewers

Sauce

1 (8-ounce) carton (1 cup) LAND O LAKES® Sour Cream (Regular, Light or No•Fat)

1/4 cup Italian dressing

1 tablespoon prepared horseradish

In large plastic food bag place sirloin pieces and 1/4 cup Italian dressing; tightly seal bag. Turn bag several times to coat sirloin well. Place in 13x9-inch pan. Refrigerate at least 30 minutes.

Meanwhile, prepare grill placing coals to one side; heat until coals are ash white. Make aluminum foil drip pan; place opposite coals. In small bowl stir together all sauce ingredients; set aside.

To assemble kabobs on metal skewers alternately thread sirloin, mushrooms, tomatoes, green pepper and onion. Place kabobs on grill over drip pan. Grill, turning occasionally, until sirloin is desired doneness (10 to 15 minutes). Serve kabobs with sauce.
YIELD: 4 servings (1 cup sauce).

Microwave Directions: Use 6 (8-inch) wooden skewers. Prepare kabobs and sauce as directed above. Place kabobs in 12x8-inch baking dish. Cover; microwave on HIGH 5 minutes. Turn kabobs; microwave on HIGH until sirloin is desired doneness (4 to 5 minutes). Serve kabobs with sauce.

Nutrition Facts (1 serving): Calories 320; Protein 26g; Carbohydrate 14g; Fat 18g; Cholesterol 80mg; Sodium 240mg

Grilled Garden Kabobs

Fresh vegetables are grilled with an herb flavor basting butter.

Preparation time: 30 minutes • Grilling time: 20 minutes

Kabobs

- 2 ears corn on the cob, husked, cut into 3 pieces
- 3 medium zucchini, cut into 4 pieces
- 1 large onion, cut into 12 wedges
- 12 large fresh mushroom caps
- 2 red or green peppers, cut into 2-inch pieces
- 6 cherry tomatoes

- 6 (12-inch) metal skewers

Butter Baste

- $1/2$ cup LAND O LAKES® Butter, melted
- $1/2$ teaspoon dried chives
- $1/2$ teaspoon dried dill weed
- $1/8$ teaspoon garlic salt
- $1/4$ teaspoon lemon juice

Prepare grill placing coals to one side; heat until coals are ash white. Make aluminum foil drip pan; place opposite coals. In 2-quart saucepan bring enough water to a full boil to cover corn. Add corn; return water to full boil. Cover; continue boiling until corn is tender (5 to 8 minutes). Drain; set aside.

To assemble kabobs on metal skewers alternately thread zucchini, onion, mushrooms and red peppers, reserving 4-inch space on end of each skewer for corn and tomato (to be added later).

In small bowl stir together all butter baste ingredients. Place kabobs on grill over drip pan. Cover; grill, turning and rotating kabobs occasionally, 10 minutes. Continue grilling, turning and brushing with butter baste occasionally, until vegetables are crisply tender (8 to 12 minutes). Using oven mitts, add corn (skewer through center of cob) and tomato to each skewer. Continue grilling until corn and tomato are heated through (2 to 3 minutes). **YIELD:** 6 servings.

Nutrition Facts (1 serving): Calories 100; Protein 4g; Carbohydrate 15g; Fat 5g; Cholesterol 10mg; Sodium 60mg

Grapefruit & Garlic Shrimp Kabobs

Grapefruit is an unusual, but tasty, ingredient in these seafood kabobs.

Preparation time: 30 minutes • Marinating time: 2 hours • Grilling time: 9 minutes

Marinade

- ¹/₂ cup grapefruit juice
- ¹/₂ cup dry white wine <u>or</u> unsweetened white grape juice
- ¹/₃ cup olive <u>or</u> vegetable oil
- ¹/₄ cup chopped fresh cilantro
- 1 teaspoon finely chopped fresh garlic
- ¹/₄ teaspoon coarsely ground pepper

Kabobs

- 1 pound (20 to 25) fresh raw shrimp, shelled, deveined, rinsed, drained
- 24 garlic cloves, blanched, skins removed
- 2 grapefruit, ends trimmed off, each cut into 4 slices, then cut into quarters

- 8 (8-inch) wooden skewers, soaked in water

In large plastic food bag place all marinade ingredients; add shrimp. Tightly seal bag. Turn bag several times to coat shrimp well. Place in 13x9-inch pan. Refrigerate at least 2 hours.

<u>Prepare grill</u>; heat until coals are ash white. Remove shrimp from marinade. To assemble kabobs on wooden skewers alternately thread shrimp, garlic cloves and grapefruit slices. Place kabobs on grill. Grill, turning once, until shrimp turn pink (9 to 11 minutes).

YIELD: 4 servings.

TIP: To blanch garlic cloves, in 2-quart saucepan bring 3 cups water to a full boil. Place garlic cloves in boiling water. Continue boiling for 3 to 4 minutes. Remove cloves from water; while warm remove skins from cloves.

Nutrition Facts (1 serving): Calories 200; Protein 19g; Carbohydrate 17g; Fat 6g; Cholesterol 130mg; Sodium 130mg

Grilled Fruit Kabobs With Coconut Cream Dip

These fresh fruit kabobs are delicious when served
with a tropical coconut cream.

Preparation time: 30 minutes • Marinating time: 1 hour • Grilling time: 5 minutes

Kabobs

- 1 (20-ounce) can chunk pineapple in juice, drained, <u>reserve juice</u>
- $2/3$ cup honey
- 1 red apple, cut into 1-inch pieces
- 1 green apple, cut into 1-inch pieces
- 2 bananas, cut into 1-inch pieces
- 12 to 16 maraschino cherries

- 8 (8-inch) wooden skewers, soaked in water

Dip

- 1 (8-ounce) carton (1 cup) LAND O LAKES® Sour Cream (Regular, Light <u>or</u> No•Fat)
- $1/2$ cup flaked coconut, toasted
- $1/2$ teaspoon vanilla

In large plastic food bag place $1/2$ cup reserved pineapple juice and honey; add pineapple and all remaining kabob ingredients <u>except</u> wooden skewers. Tightly seal bag. Turn bag several times to coat fruit well. Place in 13x9-inch pan. Refrigerate at least 1 hour to blend flavors.

Meanwhile, <u>prepare grill</u> placing coals to one side; heat until coals are ash white. Make aluminum foil drip pan; place opposite coals. To assemble kabobs on wooden skewers alternately thread fruit; <u>reserve juice and honey mixture</u>. In small bowl stir together $1/4$ cup reserved juice and honey mixture, sour cream, coconut and vanilla; set aside.

Place kabobs on grill over drip pan. Cover; grill kabobs, turning occasionally, until heated through (5 to 8 minutes). Serve with dip. **YIELD:** 8 servings ($1 1/2$ cups dip).

Nutrition Facts (1 serving): Calories 180; Protein 2g; Carbohydrate 37g; Fat 4g; Cholesterol 5mg; Sodium 35mg

Vegetable Garden Fish Kabobs

Serve with a fresh spinach salad, sourdough bread and tall glasses of iced tea for a quick, relaxing summer meal.

Preparation time: 30 minutes • Grilling time: 10 minutes

Kabobs

- 1 pound cod <u>or</u> haddock fillets, cut into 1-inch cubes
- 1 medium zucchini, cut into $1/2$-inch pieces
- 12 cherry tomatoes
- 12 medium fresh mushrooms
- 1 medium green pepper, cut into 1-inch pieces

- 6 (12-inch) metal skewers

Sauce

- $1/2$ cup LAND O LAKES® Butter, melted
- $1/4$ cup teriyaki sauce <u>or</u> soy sauce
- 2 tablespoons lemon juice

<u>Prepare grill</u> placing coals to one side; heat until coals are ash white. Make aluminum foil drip pan; place opposite coals. To assemble kabobs on metal skewers alternately thread cubes of cod, zucchini, tomatoes, mushrooms and green pepper.

In small bowl stir together all sauce ingredients; brush over kabobs. Place kabobs on grill over drip pan. Grill, turning and basting with sauce occasionally, until cod flakes with a fork (10 to 20 minutes). Serve with remaining sauce. **YIELD:** 6 servings.

Nutrition Facts (1 serving): Calories 230; Protein 16g; Carbohydrate 7g; Fat 16g; Cholesterol 75mg; Sodium 660mg

Swordfish Kabobs

Swordfish is a mild-flavored, firm, meatlike fish.

Preparation time: 30 minutes • Grilling time: 10 minutes

Kabobs

- 2 **pounds swordfish fillets, cut into 1-inch cubes***
- 2 **large lemons, each cut into 6 wedges**
- 8 **cherry tomatoes**
- 1 **medium red onion, cut into 1-inch chunks**
- 1 **medium red pepper, cut into 2-inch pieces**
- 1 **medium green pepper, cut into 2-inch pieces**

- 4 **(12-inch) metal skewers**

Sauce

- 1/3 **cup LAND O LAKES® Butter, melted**
- 1/2 **teaspoon dried basil leaves**
- 1 **teaspoon finely chopped fresh garlic**

<u>Prepare grill</u> placing coals to one side; heat until coals are ash white. Make aluminum foil drip pan; place opposite coals.

Meanwhile, in small bowl stir together all sauce ingredients; set aside.

To assemble kabobs on metal skewers alternately thread cubes of swordfish, lemons and vegetables. Place kabobs on grill over drip pan. Grill, turning and basting with sauce occasionally, until swordfish flakes with a fork (10 to 20 minutes). **YIELD:** 4 servings.

* 2 pounds cod or haddock fillets, cut into 2-inch pieces, can be substituted for 2 pounds swordfish fillets, cut into 1-inch cubes. Fold cod or haddock pieces in half before placing on skewers.

Nutrition Facts (1 serving): Calories 450; Protein 46g; Carbohydrate 10g; Fat 25g; Cholesterol 130mg; Sodium 370mg

Burgers & Sandwiches

When you want to spend less time cooking, burgers and sandwiches are the way to go! Bite into a Grilled Stuffed Cheeseburger, a Chutney Grilled Cheese & Ham Sandwich or Mixed Grill Whole Wheat Pizza. Each one of these recipes needs just a short time on the grill so you have more time for fun.

Grilled Stuffed Cheeseburger, see page 90

Grilled Stuffed Cheeseburger

Serve these cream cheese and olive-stuffed burgers with
Caesar salad and corn on the cob.

Preparation time: 30 minutes • Grilling time: 13 minutes

1 (3-ounce) package cream
   cheese, softened

1 (2¹/₂-ounce) jar sliced
   mushrooms, drained

2 tablespoons chopped green
   pepper

¹/₄ teaspoon garlic salt

¹/₈ teaspoon pepper

2 pounds ground beef

4 ounces LAND O LAKES®
   Cheddar Cheese, cut into
   16 (2x1-inch) slices

4 Kaiser rolls, cut in half

Prepare grill; heat until coals are ash white.

Meanwhile, in small bowl stir together cream cheese, mushrooms, green pepper, garlic salt and pepper. Shape ground beef into 8 large ¹/₂-inch thick patties. Place about 2 tablespoons cream cheese mixture on top of each of 4 patties. Top each with remaining meat patty; press around edges to seal. Place hamburgers on grill. Grill, turning once, until desired doneness (12 to 15 minutes). Top each hamburger with 4 slices cheese; continue grilling until cheese melts (1 minute). Serve hamburgers on rolls. **YIELD:** 4 sandwiches.

Nutrition Facts (1 sandwich): Calories 790; Protein 50g; Carbohydrate 32g; Fat 50g;
Cholesterol 190mg; Sodium 860mg

Onion Stuffed Hamburgers With Sloppy Joe Sauce

*This juicy hamburger has grilled onions for the filling
and a sloppy joe sauce on top.*

Preparation time: 30 minutes • Grilling time: 12 minutes

Hamburgers

1 tablespoon vegetable oil

1/2 cup thinly sliced onion,
   separated into rings

1 1/2 pounds ground beef

1/4 teaspoon salt

1/4 teaspoon coarsely ground
   pepper

1 tablespoon Worcestershire
   sauce

Sauce

1/3 cup coarsely chopped celery

1/4 cup ketchup

1/4 cup water

1 (6-ounce) can tomato paste

1 tablespoon firmly packed
   brown sugar

1/4 teaspoon salt

1/4 teaspoon coarsely ground
   pepper

1 tablespoon country-style
   Dijon mustard

2 tablespoons red wine
   vinegar

1 tablespoon Worcestershire
   sauce

4 onion hamburger buns

<u>Prepare grill</u>; heat until coals are ash white.

Meanwhile, in 10-inch skillet heat oil over medium heat (1 to 2 minutes); add onion. Continue cooking, stirring occasionally, until tender (3 to 4 minutes). Remove from skillet; set aside.

In medium bowl stir together all remaining hamburger ingredients. Shape into 8 large <u>1</u>/4-inch thick patties. Place <u>1</u>/4 of onion on top of each of <u>4</u> patties. Top each with remaining meat patty; press around edges to seal. Place hamburgers on grill. Grill, turning once, until desired doneness (12 to 15 minutes).

Meanwhile, in 2-quart saucepan stir together all sauce ingredients <u>except</u> buns. Cook over medium heat, stirring occasionally, until heated through (7 to 10 minutes). Place hamburgers on bottom bun halves; spoon about <u>2 tablespoons</u> sauce on hamburgers. Top with remaining bun halves. Serve with remaining sauce. **YIELD:** 4 sandwiches (2 cups sauce).

Nutrition Facts (1 sandwich): Calories 560; Protein 33g; Carbohydrate 40g; Fat 30g; Cholesterol 105mg; Sodium 1280mg

Spicy Jumbo Burger Olé

The addition of taco seasoning mix to the ground beef mixture gives this burger its spicy flavor.

Preparation time: 30 minutes • Chilling time: 30 minutes • Grilling time: 15 minutes

Hamburger
- $^1/_4$ cup dry bread crumbs
- $^1/_4$ cup finely chopped onion
- $1^1/_2$ pounds ground beef
- 1 egg, slightly beaten
- 1 ($1^1/_4$-ounce) package taco seasoning mix

- 1 (7 to 8-inch) round unsliced loaf sourdough bread, sliced in half horizontally*
  LAND O LAKES® Butter, softened

Toppings
- 4 LAND O LAKES® American Pasteurized Process Cheese Food Singles
  Shredded lettuce
  Chopped ripe tomato
  Sliced pitted ripe olives
  LAND O LAKES® Sour Cream (Regular, Light <u>or</u> No•Fat)
  Guacamole
  Salsa

<u>Prepare grill</u>; heat until coals are ash white.

Meanwhile, in large bowl combine all hamburger ingredients except bread and butter; mix well. Shape into 1 large (8 to 9-inch diameter) hamburger patty. Place on waxed paper lined cookie sheet; cover. Refrigerate at least 30 minutes.

Meanwhile, spread bread halves with butter; set aside.

Place hamburger on grill. Grill, turning once (if necessary, use two metal spatulas) until desired doneness (13 to 15 minutes).

Meanwhile, place bread halves, cut side down, alongside hamburger (not directly over coals). Grill bread, rotating occasionally, until toasted (3 to 4 minutes). Place 4 slices of cheese on hamburger; continue grilling until cheese is melted (2 to 4 minutes).

To serve, place hamburger on bottom bread half; top with lettuce, tomato, olives, sour cream, guacamole and salsa. Top with bread half. For easier serving, skewer with 6 skewers from top to bottom. Cut into 6 wedges. **YIELD**: 6 servings.

* If loaf of bread is too tall, slice into 3 horizontal layers. Remove center layer for other use.

TIP: If desired, jumbo burger can be made into 6 individual hamburgers and served on 6 hamburger buns. Shape hamburger mixture into 6 patties. Place hamburgers on grill. Grill, turning once, until desired doneness (12 to 15 minutes). Top with 1 slice cheese. Continue grilling until cheese is melted (about 1 minute). Toast buns and serve as directed above.

Nutrition Facts (1 serving): Calories 560; Protein 31g; Carbohydrate 50g; Fat 26g; Cholesterol 130mg; Sodium 1160mg

Hamburgers With Cucumber Relish

This relish, made with thinly sliced cucumber, tomatoes and red onion, tastes great on grilled hamburgers.

Preparation time: 30 minutes • Grilling time: 10 minutes

Hamburgers
$1^1/_2$ pounds ground beef
$^1/_4$ cup chopped onion
$^1/_4$ teaspoon salt
$^1/_4$ teaspoon pepper
 2 tablespoons country-style Dijon mustard

Relish
 1 teaspoon dill seed
 1 teaspoon mustard seed
 2 tablespoons cider vinegar
 1 tablespoon vegetable oil
 1 tablespoon country-style Dijon mustard
 1 medium (1 cup) cucumber, thinly sliced
 2 medium (1 cup) ripe tomatoes, thinly sliced
 1 small (1 cup) red onion, thinly sliced, separated into rings

Prepare grill; heat until coals are ash white.

Meanwhile, in medium bowl stir together ground beef, onion, salt, pepper and 2 tablespoons mustard. Form into 6 large $^1/_4$-inch thick patties; set aside.

In medium bowl combine all relish ingredients except cucumbers, tomatoes and onion. Add vegetables; toss to coat. Place hamburgers on grill. Grill, turning once, until desired doneness (10 to 15 minutes for medium). Spoon relish on hamburgers. **YIELD:** 6 servings.

Nutrition Facts (1 serving): Calories 270; Protein 19g; Carbohydrate 5g; Fat 19g; Cholesterol 70mg; Sodium 380mg

Spinach & Swiss Cheese Stuffed Hamburgers

The spinach and cheese stuffing keeps these burgers extra moist.

Preparation time: 15 minutes • Cooking time: 30 minutes • Grilling time: 12 minutes

Sauce

- 1 (14-ounce) bottle (1^1/$_2$ cups) ketchup
- 1 large (1 cup) onion, chopped
- ^{1}/$_2$ cup sliced ^{1}/$_8$-inch green pepper
- ^{1}/$_4$ cup currant jelly
- ^{1}/$_4$ teaspoon dry mustard
- 1 teaspoon prepared horseradish
- 1 tablespoon cider vinegar

Hamburgers

- 4 ounces (1 cup) LAND O LAKES® Swiss Cheese, shredded
- 1^1/$_2$ pounds lean ground beef
- 1 (10-ounce) package frozen chopped spinach, thawed, well drained, pressed with paper towels
- ^{1}/$_2$ teaspoon coarsely ground pepper
- 1 teaspoon finely chopped fresh garlic

- 6 hamburger buns

Prepare grill; heat until coals are ash white.

Meanwhile, in 2-quart saucepan stir together all sauce ingredients. Cook over medium heat, stirring occasionally, until mixture comes to a full boil (10 to 12 minutes). Reduce heat to medium low. Continue cooking, stirring occasionally, until sauce thickens slightly and flavors are blended (20 to 30 minutes).

Meanwhile, in large bowl stir together all hamburger ingredients <u>except</u> buns. Shape into 6 (^{3}/$_4$-inch) thick patties. Place hamburgers on grill. Grill, turning once, until desired doneness (12 to 18 minutes). Serve hamburgers on buns; top with sauce. **YIELD:** 6 sandwiches (2 cups sauce).

Nutrition Facts (1 sandwich): Calories 540; Protein 31g; Carbohydrate 54g; Fat 23g; Cholesterol 90mg; Sodium 1140mg

Mixed Grill Whole Wheat Pizza

*Have your family choose the toppings to create
a delicious and colorful pizza.*

Preparation time: 30 minutes • Standing time: 20 minutes • Rising time: 15 minutes • Grilling time: 22 minutes

Crust

- 1 (^{1}/4-ounce) package active dry yeast
- 1 cup warm water (105 to 115°F)
- 1 teaspoon sugar
- ^{1}/2 teaspoon salt
- 2 tablespoons olive <u>or</u> vegetable oil
- 1^1/4 to 1^1/2 cups all-purpose flour
- 1 cup whole wheat flour

Sauce

- 1 (8-ounce) can tomato sauce
- 1 (6-ounce) can tomato paste
- 2 teaspoons dried basil leaves
- ^{1}/2 teaspoon dried oregano leaves
- ^{1}/4 teaspoon coarsely ground pepper

Toppings

- 1 medium (1 cup) onion, thinly sliced, separated into rings
- 10 ounces (2^1/2 cups) LAND O LAKES® Mozzarella Cheese, shredded
- Marinated artichokes, drained, quartered
- Pitted ripe or green olives
- Red <u>or</u> green pepper, cut into thin julienne strips
- Sauteed mushrooms
- Browned Italian sausage
- ^{1}/4 cup freshly grated Parmesan cheese

In large bowl dissolve yeast in warm water; stir in sugar, salt and oil. Gradually stir in all-purpose flour and whole wheat flour to make soft dough. Turn dough onto lightly floured surface; knead 10 to 15 times. Place in greased bowl; turn greased side up. Cover; let stand 20 minutes.

Meanwhile, in medium bowl stir together all sauce ingredients. <u>Prepare grill</u> placing coals on both sides; heat until coals are ash white. Place sheets of aluminum foil on grill in center.

Using greased or floured fingers press dough into 15x10-inch rectangle on large greased cookie sheet. Cover; let rise for 15 to 20 minutes.

Place cookie sheet on aluminum foil on grill. Grill until lightly browned (10 to 14 minutes). Remove from grill. Spread sauce to within ^{1}/2 inch of outside edge of crust. Top with onion rings and <u>2 cups</u> Mozzarella cheese. Sprinkle with choice of topping ingredients. Sprinkle with remaining ^{1}/2 cup Mozzarella cheese and Parmesan cheese. Place cookie sheet with pizza on aluminum foil on grill. Grill, covered, until pizza crust is done and cheese is melted (12 to 17 minutes). **YIELD:** 6 servings.

Nutrition Facts (1 serving without toppings): Calories 400; Protein 22g; Carbohydrate 46g; Fat 15g; Cholesterol 30mg; Sodium 960mg

Barbecue Pork Sandwiches

This barbecued shredded pork can be kept refrigerated and reheated in the microwave oven for a quick sandwich-on-the-run.

Preparation time: 15 minutes • Cooking time: 2 hours 21 minutes

Pork

2 pounds boneless pork shoulder roast

1 medium ($\frac{1}{2}$ cup) onion, chopped

2 teaspoons finely chopped fresh garlic

$\frac{1}{2}$ cup water

Sauce

1 (14-ounce) bottle ($1\frac{1}{2}$ cups) ketchup

1 tablespoon chili powder

1 teaspoon firmly packed brown sugar

$\frac{1}{4}$ teaspoon coarsely ground pepper

1 tablespoon country-style Dijon mustard

3 tablespoons Worcestershire sauce

2 tablespoons cider vinegar

9 hamburger buns

Heat oven to 325°. In roasting pan place pork roast. Sprinkle with onion and garlic; add water. Cover; bake until roast shreds easily with fork (2 to 2$\frac{1}{2}$ hours). Remove from pan. <u>Reserve pan juices</u>; skim off fat. With fork shred roast into small pieces.

In 3-quart saucepan combine all sauce ingredients and reserved pan juices. Cook over medium heat, stirring occasionally, until sauce comes to a full boil (6 to 8 minutes). Reduce heat to low; continue cooking 10 minutes. Stir in shredded pork. Continue cooking until heated through (5 to 8 minutes). **YIELD:** 9 sandwiches.

Nutrition Facts (1 sandwich): Calories 290; Protein 17g; Carbohydrate 36g; Fat 9g; Cholesterol 45mg; Sodium 850mg

Chutney Grilled Cheese & Ham

*A slightly sweet, fruity chutney will taste best in this
hot cheese and ham sandwich.*

Preparation time: 30 minutes • Grilling time: 2 minutes

4 (½-inch center cut) slices
   (from 1 pound round loaf)
   sourdough bread

½ cup chutney

12 (2¼x1⅛-inch) slices
   LAND O LAKES® Swiss
   Cheese

4 ounces thinly sliced cooked
   ham

3 tablespoons LAND O LAKES®
   Butter, softened

<u>Prepare grill</u>; heat until coals are ash white.

Meanwhile, spread <u>1</u> side of each bread slice with chutney. To assemble
each sandwich layer <u>1</u> bread slice with <u>3 slices</u> cheese, <u>½</u> of ham,
<u>3 slices</u> cheese and <u>1</u> bread slice. Lightly spread butter on both sides of
sandwiches. Place sandwiches on grill. Grill, turning once, until golden
brown (2 to 5 minutes). **YIELD:** 4 sandwiches.

*Nutrition Facts (1 sandwich): Calories 500; Protein 27g; Carbohydrate 43g; Fat 23g;
Cholesterol 85mg; Sodium 1030mg*

Grilled Sausage Patties On Rye

Lots of Mozzarella cheese melts between sausage patties,
onions and grilled caraway rye bread.

Preparation time: 30 minutes • Grilling time: 9 minutes

1 pound pork sausage

1 tablespoon vegetable oil

1 medium onion, sliced
    $1/8$-inch

8 green pepper rings

8 (1-ounce) slices
    LAND O LAKES®
    Mozzarella Cheese

8 slices caraway rye bread

$1/4$ cup LAND O LAKES®
    Butter, softened

Prepare grill; heat until coals are ash white.

Meanwhile, form sausage into 8 patties; place on grill. Grill, turning once, until browned and cooked through (6 to 8 minutes).

Meanwhile, in 10-inch skillet heat oil; add onion and green pepper. Cook over medium heat, stirring occasionally, until vegetables are crisply tender (4 to 5 minutes). Remove vegetables from skillet; drain. To assemble each sandwich place 1 slice cheese on slice of bread. Top with 2 sausage patties, $1/4$ of onion slices, 2 green pepper rings, 1 slice cheese and 1 slice of bread. Spread softened butter on outside of sandwiches. Place sandwiches on grill. Grill, turning once, until golden brown and cheese is melted (3 to 5 minutes). **YIELD:** 4 sandwiches.

Nutrition Facts (1 sandwich): Calories 620; Protein 31g; Carbohydrate 32g; Fat 42g;
Cholesterol 105mg; Sodium 1390mg

On the Side

Grilled meals deserve special side dishes to complement their flavors and textures. So we've collected some unique recipes to make your meals complete. Try tangy Blue Cheese Coleslaw, warm Cheese & Herb Grilled Bread or spicy Old-World Potato Salad for delicious results!

Lemon Zest Dressing Over Fresh Fruit, see page 104

Lemon Zest Dressing Over Fresh Fruit

A light lemonade dressing is drizzled over sliced pineapple, strawberries and kiwi.

Preparation time: 20 minutes

¼ cup lemon juice

2 teaspoons sugar

1 teaspoon grated lemon peel

6 (¼-inch) slices fresh pineapple, peeled, cored

1 pint strawberries, hulled, sliced ¼-inch

1 kiwi fruit, peeled, sliced ⅛-inch, cut in half

In small bowl stir together lemon juice, sugar and lemon peel. On individual salad plates place <u>1 slice</u> pineapple; divide strawberries and kiwi evenly between salad plates. Spoon about <u>2 teaspoons</u> dressing over each serving. **YIELD:** 6 servings.

TIP: Dressing can be used on your favorite combination of fruits.

Nutrition Facts (1 serving): Calories 70; Protein 1g; Carbohydrate 18g; Fat 1g; Cholesterol 0mg; Sodium 4mg

Cucumbers In Country Cream

This cool, crisp cucumber salad has a delicate lemon flavor.

Preparation time: 20 minutes • Chilling time: 1 hour

¹/₂ cup LAND O LAKES® Sour Cream (Regular, Light <u>or</u> No•Fat)	
2 tablespoons finely chopped onion	
¹/₄ teaspoon salt	
¹/₄ teaspoon paprika	
¹/₈ teaspoon garlic powder	
Dash pepper	
1 tablespoon lemon juice	
2 medium cucumbers, peeled, sliced	

In medium bowl stir together all ingredients <u>except</u> cucumbers; refrigerate at least 1 hour. Just before serving, gently stir in cucumbers.
YIELD: 6 servings.

Nutrition Facts (1 serving): Calories 35; Protein 2g; Carbohydrate 5g; Fat 1g; Cholesterol 5mg; Sodium 105mg

Tomato & Cucumber In Vinaigrette

*Plump, ripe tomatoes and refreshing, crisp cucumbers pair up in
this fresh-from-the-garden salad.*

Preparation time: 30 minutes

Vinaigrette

- ¹/₃ cup olive <u>or</u> vegetable oil
- 1 tablespoon chopped fresh chives*
- 1 teaspoon chopped fresh mint leaves**
- ¹/₂ teaspoon sugar
- ¹/₄ teaspoon salt
- ¹/₄ teaspoon pepper
- 2 tablespoons red wine vinegar

Salad

- 6 Boston lettuce leaves, radicchio leaves <u>or</u> leaf lettuce leaves
- 3 ripe tomatoes, cut into ¹/₄-inch slices
- 1 medium cucumber, cut into ¹/₄-inch slices
- ¹/₂ cup sliced pitted ripe olives

In jar with tight-fitting lid combine all vinaigrette ingredients; shake well. Refrigerate until ready to serve.

On individual salad or dinner plates place <u>1</u> lettuce leaf. Arrange <u>3 to 4 slices</u> tomato and <u>4 to 5 slices</u> cucumber on each lettuce leaf. Sprinkle with olives. Just before serving, drizzle with vinaigrette. **YIELD:** 6 servings.

*1 teaspoon dried chives can be substituted for 1 tablespoon chopped fresh chives.

**¹/₄ teaspoon dried mint leaves can be substituted for 1 teaspoon chopped fresh mint leaves.

Nutrition Facts (1 serving): Calories 140; Protein 1g; Carbohydrate 4g; Fat 14g; Cholesterol 0mg; Sodium 190mg

Stove Top Spicy Baked Beans

Salsa adds a southwestern flair to these stove top baked beans.

Preparation time: 20 minutes • Cooking time: 48 minutes

3 (16-ounce) cans baked
   beans

1 (16-ounce) jar (2 cups)
   medium salsa

1 pound hickory smoked
   bacon, cooked, crumbled

1 cup chopped red onion

$1/4$ cup firmly packed brown
   sugar

$1/4$ cup chopped fresh parsley

2 tablespoons stone ground
   mustard

2 tablespoons light molasses

1 teaspoon finely chopped
   fresh garlic

2 tablespoons red wine
   vinegar

In 3-quart saucepan combine all ingredients. Cook over medium heat, stirring occasionally, until beans come to a full boil (8 to 12 minutes). Reduce heat to low; continue cooking, stirring occasionally, until flavors blend (40 to 45 minutes). **YIELD:** 12 servings.

Nutrition Facts (1 serving): Calories 230; Protein 9g; Carbohydrate 33g; Fat 7g; Cholesterol 15mg; Sodium 930mg

Corn On The Cob With Seasoned Butters

This corn on the cob tastes great with grilled hamburgers,
baked beans and relishes.

Preparation time: 30 minutes • Grilling time: 20 minutes

$1/2$ cup LAND O LAKES®
   Butter, softened

Dill Butter
2 teaspoons dried chives
1 teaspoon dried dill weed
1 teaspoon lemon juice

Italian Butter
$1/4$ teaspoon dried basil leaves
$1/4$ teaspoon dried oregano
   leaves
$1/4$ teaspoon garlic salt

Horseradish Parsley Butter
1 tablespoon chopped fresh
   parsley
$1/4$ teaspoon salt
$1/8$ teaspoon pepper
2 teaspoons prepared
   horseradish

Sesame Mustard Butter
2 tablespoons sesame seed,
   toasted
$1/4$ teaspoon salt
$1/4$ teaspoon dry mustard
$1/8$ teaspoon pepper

Corn on the cob, husked

In small mixer bowl combine butter and all ingredients for desired seasoned butter. Beat at medium speed, scraping bowl often, until light and fluffy (1 to 2 minutes). Serve butter at room temperature with hot sweet corn. **YIELD:** $1/2$ cup butter.

Grilling Directions: Prepare grill; heat until coals are ash white. Spread about 1 tablespoon desired seasoned butter evenly over each ear of corn. Wrap each ear of corn tightly in heavy-duty double thickness aluminum foil; seal well. Place on grill directly over coals. Grill, turning every 5 minutes, until tender (20 to 25 minutes).

Stove Top Directions: In 5-quart Dutch oven bring enough water to a full boil to cover corn. Add corn; return water to full boil. Cover; continue boiling until corn is tender (5 to 8 minutes).

Microwave Directions: In ungreased 12x8-inch baking dish combine $1/4$ cup water and 4 ears of corn. Cover with plastic food wrap; microwave on HIGH, rearranging corn every 3 minutes, until corn is tender (10 to 11 minutes). Let stand 4 minutes; drain.

Nutrition Facts (1 teaspoon Dill Butter only): Calories 35; Protein 0g; Carbohydrate 0g; Fat 4g; Cholesterol 10mg; Sodium 40mg

Shrimp Dilled Deviled Eggs

Place these shrimp and dill-seasoned deviled eggs in a plastic food wrap lined egg carton for easy carrying to a picnic or barbecue.

Preparation time: 30 minutes

6   hard-cooked eggs, peeled
1/4 cup mayonnaise
1   (4¼-ounce) can deveined medium shrimp, rinsed, drained, <u>reserve 12 shrimp</u>
2   tablespoons chopped green onions
1   tablespoon chopped fresh dill*
1/8 teaspoon pepper
2   teaspoons country-style Dijon mustard
1   tablespoon lime juice
1/4 teaspoon hot pepper sauce

Fresh dill

Cut eggs crosswise in half. Remove yolks from egg whites; set egg whites aside. Place cooked egg yolks in medium bowl; mash with fork. Add mayonnaise, shrimp, onions, 1 tablespoon dill, pepper, mustard, lime juice and hot pepper sauce to egg yolks; stir to blend. Spoon about 1 tablespoon egg yolk mixture into each egg white; garnish with reserved shrimp and sprig of dill. Cover; refrigerate. **YIELD:** 1 dozen.

* 1 teaspoon dried dill weed can be substituted for 1 tablespoon chopped fresh dill.

Nutrition Facts (1 egg): Calories 90; Protein 5g; Carbohydrate 1g; Fat 7g; Cholesterol 125mg; Sodium 85mg

Pineapple Pepper Dip

Assorted bell peppers, pineapple and fresh lime add color to this refreshing dip.

Preparation time: 30 minutes • Chilling time: 1 hour

1 cup chopped assorted bell peppers (green, red and yellow)

8 ounces (1 cup) LAND O LAKES® Sour Cream (Regular, Light <u>or</u> No•Fat)

1 (8-ounce) package cream cheese, softened

1 (8-ounce) can crushed pineapple, well drained

$1/8$ teaspoon salt

2 tablespoons coarsely chopped fresh cilantro <u>or</u> parsley

2 tablespoons chopped green onion

2 teaspoons finely chopped seeded jalapeño pepper

1 teaspoon grated lime peel

1 teaspoon lime juice

Fresh vegetable sticks (pepper, celery, carrot, cucumber, etc.)

Tortilla chips

In small mixer bowl combine all ingredients <u>except</u> vegetable sticks and tortilla chips. Beat at medium speed, scraping bowl often, until well mixed (1 to 2 minutes). Cover; refrigerate at least 1 hour. Serve with fresh vegetable sticks or tortilla chips. **YIELD:** $3^1/4$ cups.

Nutrition Facts (1 tablespoon): Calories 22; Protein 1g; Carbohydrate 1g; Fat 2g; Cholesterol 5mg; Sodium 25mg

Crunchy Cabbage Salad

Colorful vegetables mixed with crunchy noodles and a tangy dressing make a delightful salad.

Preparation time: 20 minutes

Dressing

 1/4 cup vegetable oil
  2 tablespoons sugar
 1/4 teaspoon salt
 1/4 teaspoon pepper
  3 tablespoons red wine
     vinegar

Salad

  3 cups shredded green
     cabbage
  3 cups shredded red cabbage
  2 medium (1 cup) carrots,
     shredded
  3 tablespoons sliced green
     onions
 3/4 cup salted peanuts
  1 (3-ounce) package uncooked
     chicken-flavored ramen
     noodle soup

In small bowl stir together all dressing ingredients; set aside.

In large bowl toss together green cabbage, red cabbage, carrots, green onions and <u>1/2 cup</u> peanuts. Sprinkle dry soup seasoning packet over salad. Break noodles into small pieces; stir into salad. Pour dressing over salad; toss to coat. Sprinkle with remaining peanuts.
YIELD: 8 servings.

TIP: If softer noodles are preferred, salad can be prepared up to 4 hours ahead. Cover; refrigerate until ready to serve.

Nutrition Facts (1 serving): Calories 220; Protein 6g; Carbohydrate 18g; Fat 15g; Cholesterol 0mg; Sodium 440mg

Blue Cheese Coleslaw

Coleslaw becomes special with a touch of blue cheese for an enticing flavor difference.

Preparation time: 30 minutes • Chilling time: 1 hour

Dressing

- $1/2$ cup (4 ounces) crumbled blue cheese
- $1/4$ cup sugar
- 1 cup mayonnaise
- $1/2$ teaspoon celery seed
- $1/2$ teaspoon garlic salt
- 1 tablespoon prepared mustard
- 2 tablespoons vinegar

Coleslaw

- 8 cups shredded cabbage
- 2 medium (1 cup) carrots, shredded
- $1/4$ cup sliced green onions

- 1 cup cherry tomato halves, if desired

In medium bowl stir together $1/4$ cup blue cheese and all remaining dressing ingredients. Cover; refrigerate at least 1 hour.

Just before serving, in large bowl combine cabbage, carrots and green onions; add dressing. Toss gently to coat. Sprinkle remaining $1/4$ cup blue cheese on top of coleslaw. Arrange cherry tomatoes around edge of bowl. (Serve within 2 hours of combining coleslaw with dressing.)

YIELD: 12 servings.

Nutrition Facts (1 serving): Calories 200; Protein 3g; Carbohydrate 9g; Fat 18g; Cholesterol 20mg; Sodium 340mg

Potato, Cucumber & Onion Salad

This is a very colorful, refreshing vinaigrette potato salad, perfect for a summer supper.

Preparation time: 30 minutes • Standing time: 3 hours • Chilling time: 1 hour

Salad

2 large (3 cups) cucumbers, thinly sliced

1 small (1 cup) onion, thinly sliced

1 tablespoon salt

4 large (4 cups) russet potatoes, cooked, cut into 1-inch cubes

2 cups cherry tomato halves

Dressing

1/3 cup vegetable oil

1/3 cup white wine vinegar

1 teaspoon dried basil leaves

1/4 teaspoon coarsely ground pepper

In large bowl combine cucumber, onion and salt; mix well. Cover; let stand at room temperature, stirring occasionally, 3 to 4 hours.

Place cucumber mixture in strainer; drain. Press cucumbers with paper towels to remove excess moisture. Place cucumber mixture in large bowl. Add potatoes and cherry tomatoes.

In small bowl combine all dressing ingredients. Pour over cucumber mixture; toss to coat well. Cover; refrigerate at least 1 hour to blend flavors. **YIELD:** 8 servings.

Nutrition Facts (1 serving): Calories 160; Protein 2g; Carbohydrate 18g; Fat 9g; Cholesterol 0mg; Sodium 280mg

Old-World Potato Salad

*Carrot slices, green pepper and sour cream add a touch of difference
to this creamy potato salad.*

Preparation time: 30 minutes • Chilling time: 3 hours

2 pounds (3 to 5 medium)
   russet potatoes, cooked,
   peeled, sliced

3/4 cup sliced 1/4-inch carrots

1/2 cup chopped green pepper

1 1/2 cups LAND O LAKES® Sour
   Cream (Regular, Light <u>or</u>
   No•Fat)

1 tablespoon sugar

1 teaspoon salt

1/2 teaspoon dried dill weed

1/4 teaspoon pepper

2 teaspoons prepared mustard

2 tablespoons vinegar

In large bowl combine potatoes, carrots and green pepper. In medium bowl stir together all remaining ingredients. Add to potato mixture; stir to coat well. Refrigerate at least 3 hours. **YIELD:** 6 servings.

*Nutrition Facts (1 serving): Calories 210; Protein 6g; Carbohydrate 38g; Fat 4g;
Cholesterol 15mg; Sodium 440mg*

Parmesan Potato & Carrot Bundles

Prepare bundles ahead of time, then grill at mealtime.

Preparation time: 30 minutes • Grilling time: 45 minutes

4 (14x12-inch) pieces heavy-duty aluminum foil

4 medium sliced $^1/8$-inch baking potatoes

4 medium (2 cups) carrots, cut into julienne strips

1 medium (1 cup) green pepper, cut into 1-inch pieces

1 small onion, sliced

$^1/4$ cup freshly grated Parmesan cheese

1 teaspoon garlic powder

1 teaspoon salt

$^1/2$ teaspoon pepper

$^1/2$ cup LAND O LAKES® Butter

Prepare grill; heat until coals are ash white.

Meanwhile, on each piece of aluminum foil place 1 sliced potato, $^1/2$ cup carrots, $^1/4$ cup green pepper and several slices of onion. Sprinkle each potato bundle with 1 tablespoon Parmesan cheese, $^1/4$ teaspoon salt, $^1/4$ teaspoon garlic powder and $^1/8$ teaspoon pepper; place 2 tablespoons butter on top of vegetables. Bring edges of aluminum foil up to center; tightly seal top and sides. Place bundles on grill. Cover; grill, turning after half the time, until potatoes are fork tender (45 to 55 minutes). Open bundles carefully.
YIELD: 4 servings.

Oven Directions: Heat oven to 400°. Prepare bundles as directed above. Place bundles in 13x9-inch baking pan. Bake, turning bundles after 30 minutes, for 45 to 60 minutes or until potatoes are fork tender. Open bundles carefully.

Nutrition Facts (1 serving): Calories 390; Protein 7g; Carbohydrate 37g; Fat 25g; Cholesterol 65mg; Sodium 920mg

Grilled Sourdough Bread With Garden Tomatoes

This bread uses the season's finest garden ripened tomatoes and fresh sweet basil leaves.

Preparation time: 30 minutes • Grilling time: 3 minutes

1/4 cup LAND O LAKES® Butter

2 tablespoons chopped shallots <u>or</u> onion

1/2 teaspoon finely chopped fresh garlic

4 (1/2-inch) slices round sourdough bread

1/4 cup torn fresh basil leaves

2 medium ripe tomatoes, each cut into 6 slices

2 teaspoons red wine vinegar
Salt and coarsely ground pepper

<u>Prepare grill</u>; heat until coals are ash white.

Meanwhile, in 1-quart saucepan melt butter until sizzling; stir in shallots and garlic. Cook over medium heat, stirring occasionally, until shallots are tender (1 to 2 minutes). Place bread slices on grill. Grill until toasted (2 to 3 minutes). Turn; brush each bread slice with butter mixture. Sprinkle with basil; top each bread slice with <u>3</u> tomato slices. Sprinkle each with 1/2 teaspoon vinegar; season with salt and pepper. Continue grilling until bread is lightly browned (1 to 2 minutes). **YIELD:** 4 servings.

Nutrition Facts (1 serving): Calories 220; Protein 4g; Carbohydrate 22g; Fat 13g; Cholesterol 30mg; Sodium 330mg

Cheese & Herb Grilled Bread

*Serve as a snack or with meals. Prepare ample amounts,
as it is sure to disappear quickly.*

Preparation time: 30 minutes • Grilling time: 15 minutes

Spread

3 ounces ($^3/4$ cup)
   LAND O LAKES® Cheddar
   Cheese, finely shredded
$^1/2$ cup LAND O LAKES®
   Butter, softened
$^1/4$ cup chopped fresh parsley
1 teaspoon paprika
$^1/2$ teaspoon garlic powder

Bread

1 loaf crusty French or Italian
   bread, sliced diagonally
   $^3/4$-inch

   Heavy-duty aluminum foil

<u>Prepare grill</u> placing coals to one side; heat until coals are ash white.

Meanwhile, in small bowl stir together all spread ingredients. Spread between bread slices. Wrap bread in aluminum foil, tightly sealing top and ends. Place bread on grill opposite coals. Cover; grill, turning over after half the time, until cheese is melted (15 to 20 minutes).
YIELD: 12 servings.

<u>Oven Directions</u>: Heat oven to 400°. Prepare bread as directed above. Wrap bread in aluminum foil, tightly sealing top and ends. Bake for 15 to 20 minutes or until cheese is melted.

Nutrition Facts (1 serving): Calories 210; Protein 5g; Carbohydrate 21g; Fat 11g; Cholesterol 30mg; Sodium 340mg

Summer Squash Salad

A hearty fresh zucchini, yellow squash and ripe tomato salad with a splash of Parmesan dressing.

Preparation time: 20 minutes

2 medium (2 cups) zucchini, sliced $\frac{1}{8}$-inch

2 medium (2 cups) yellow squash, sliced $\frac{1}{8}$-inch, halved lengthwise

$\frac{1}{4}$ cup freshly grated Parmesan cheese

$\frac{1}{4}$ cup cider vinegar

$\frac{1}{4}$ teaspoon salt

$\frac{1}{4}$ teaspoon dried basil leaves

$\frac{1}{4}$ teaspoon pepper

$\frac{1}{2}$ teaspoon finely chopped fresh garlic

2 tablespoons vegetable oil

$\frac{1}{2}$ cup sliced $\frac{1}{8}$-inch red onion, separated into rings

2 medium ripe tomatoes, cut into wedges

In 2-quart saucepan place zucchini and yellow squash; add enough water to cover. Cook over medium high heat until water comes to a full boil. Boil for 1 to 2 minutes; drain. Rinse with cold water; set aside.

In large bowl stir together all remaining ingredients <u>except</u> onion and tomatoes. Add zucchini, yellow squash, onion and tomatoes; toss to coat. **YIELD:** 6 servings.

Nutrition Facts (1 serving): Calories 90; Protein 3g; Carbohydrate 7g; Fat 6g; Cholesterol 5mg; Sodium 170mg

Sparkling Pink Lemonade

Spending a hot day on the front porch is just not the same without homemade lemonade–especially when it's sparkling pink!

Preparation time: 10 minutes • Chilling time: 30 minutes

1½ cups sugar

1½ cups (6 lemons) freshly
     squeezed lemon juice

1   quart (4 cups) club soda,
     chilled*

4   teaspoons grenadine
     syrup**
     6-inch wooden skewers
     Fresh fruit pieces
     (strawberries, melon balls,
     pineapple chunks, etc.)

In 2-quart pitcher combine sugar and lemon juice. Stir well; refrigerate at least 30 minutes.

Just before serving, add club soda. Stir in grenadine syrup. On 6-inch wooden skewers, thread fruit pieces to make kabobs. Place kabobs in glasses; add ice. Pour in lemonade. **YIELD:** 6 servings.

*1 quart (4 cups) water can be substituted for club soda.

**4 to 6 drops red food coloring can be substituted for grenadine syrup.

Nutrition Facts (1 serving): Calories 220; Protein 0g; Carbohydrate 58g; Fat 0g; Cholesterol 0mg; Sodium 35mg

Index

A

APPLE
Grilled Ham With Apple Chutney.............45

APRICOT
Apricot Glazed Chicken Breasts.................34

B

BEANS
Stove Top Spicy Baked Beans...................108

BEEF
Beef Kabobs With Horseradish Sauce.........80
Beef Tenderloin In Sesame Marinade..........52
Cheddar Cheese-Pecan Rolled
    Flank Steak.....................................50
Flank Steak In Fajita Marinade..................48
Grilled Beef & Pepper Bundles...................53
Grilled Steaks With Garden Tomato
    Basil Sauce.....................................54
Sweet & Tangy Family Steak.....................46
Western Barbecued Rib Sampler.................74

BEER
Western Barbecued Rib Sampler.................74

BEVERAGE
Sparkling Pink Lemonade.........................124

BLUE CHEESE
Blue Cheese Coleslaw..............................115

BOURBON
Pork Tenderloin With
    Bourbon Marinade.............................44

BREAD
Cheese & Herb Grilled Bread...................122
Grilled Sourdough Bread With Garden
    Tomatos..120
Mixed Grill Whole Wheat Pizza.................97

BUTTER
Corn On The Cob With Seasoned
    Butters...110

C

CABBAGE
Blue Cheese Coleslaw..............................115
Crunchy Cabbage Salad...........................114

CARROT
Parmesan Potato & Carrot Bundles..........119

CHEESE
Cheddar Cheese-Pecan Rolled
    Flank Steak.....................................50
Cheese & Herb Grilled Bread...................122
Chicken Breasts Southwestern...................30
Chicken Vinaigrette Salad.........................32
Chutney Grilled Cheese & Ham...............100
Grilled Beef & Pepper Bundles...................53
Grilled Fish Florentine..............................66
Grilled Garden Vegetables & Sole..............59
Grilled Sausage Patties On Rye.................101
Grilled Stuffed Cheeseburger.....................90
Mixed Grill Whole Wheat Pizza................97
Spinach & Swiss Cheese Stuffed
    Hamburgers.....................................96

CHICKEN
Apricot Glazed Chicken Breasts.................34
Chicken Breasts Southwestern...................30
Chicken Vinaigrette Salad.........................32
Company's Coming Kabobs......................79
Glazed Chicken & Orange Salsa.................22
Grilled Drumsticks With Zesty Dippers.....28
Grilled Garlic Chicken.............................29
Grilled Lemonade Drummies....................25
Peanut Chicken......................................24
Pineapple-Tarragon Chicken Breasts..........35
Tangy Grilled Chicken.............................26
Teriyaki Chicken Kabobs..........................78

CHILI
Coconut Chili Marinade...........................15

CHOPS
Mint Pesto Lamb Chops..........................38
Pork Chops With Green
    Peppercorn Sauce.............................42

CHUTNEY
Chutney Grilled Cheese & Ham...............100
Grilled Ham With Apple Chutney.............45
Pork Roast With Rhubarb Chutney...........40

CITRUS
Citrus Marinade.......................................8

COCONUT
Coconut Chili Marinade...........................15

Grilled Fruit Kabobs
    With Coconut Cream Dip....................84

COLESLAW
Blue Cheese Coleslaw..............................115

CORN
Corn On The Cob   With
    Seasoned Butters...............................110

CORNISH HEN
Herbed Hickory-Smoked Cornish Hens....18

CUCUMBER
Cucumbers In Country Cream.................105
East Indian Turkey Drumsticks...................19
Hamburgers With Cucumber Relish..........94
Potato, Cucumber & Onion Salad...........116
Rainbow Trout With Crunchy Gazpacho...60
Tomato & Cucumber In Vinaigrette.........106

CURRY
Curry Marinade.......................................12

D

DIP
Grilled Drumsticks With Zesty Dippers.....28
Grilled Fruit Kabobs
    With Coconut Cream Dip....................84
Pineapple Pepper Dip..............................112

DRUMSTICKS
East Indian Turkey Drumsticks...................19
Grilled Drumsticks With Zesty Dippers.....28
Grilled Lemonade Drummies....................25

E

EGG
Shrimp Dilled Deviled Eggs.....................111

F

FAJITA
Flank Steak In Fajita Marinade..................48

FISH
Fish Steaks With Sweet Red
    Pepper Puree....................................62
Grilled Fish Florentine..............................66
Grilled Garden Vegetables & Sole..............59
Grilled Salmon With Tarragon Butter.........64

Rainbow Trout With Crunchy Gazpacho ...60
Sea Bass With Mango Lime Salsa 67
Swordfish Kabob...................................87
Swordfish With Peach Pepper Salsa............58
Vegetable Garden Fish Kabobs...................86

FRUIT

Grilled Fruit Kabobs With Coconut
Cream Dip..84
Lemon Zest Dressing Over Fresh Fruit.....104

G

GARLIC

Grapefruit & Garlic Shrimp Kabobs...........83
Grilled Garlic Chicken 29

GAZPACHO

Rainbow Trout With Crunchy Gazpacho ...60

GLAZE

Glazed Chicken & Orange Salsa.................22
Honey Mustard Glazed Ribs 72

GRAPEFRUIT

Grapefruit & Garlic Shrimp Kabobs...........83

H

HAM

Chutney Grilled Cheese & Ham...............100
Grilled Ham With Apple Chutney.............45

HAMBURGERS

Grilled Stuffed Cheeseburger 90
Hamburgers With Cucumber Relish 94
Onion Stuffed Hamburgers With Sloppy
Joe Sauce...91
Spicy Jumbo Burger Olé 92
Spinach & Swiss Cheese
Stuffed Hamburgers 96

HONEY

Honey Mustard Glazed Ribs 72

HORSERADISH

Beef Kabobs With Horseradish Sauce 80
Grilled Drumsticks With Zesty Dippers 28

J

JUNIPER BERRY

Spicy Salsa Verde & Juniper   Berry
Marinade 14

K

KABOB

Beef Kabobs With Horseradish Sauce 80
Company's Coming Kabobs........................79
Grapefruit & Garlic Shrimp Kabobs...........83

Grilled Fruit Kabobs
With Coconut Cream Dip 84
Grilled Garden Kabobs 82
Spicy Cajun Shrimp...................................68
Swordfish Kabobs.....................................87
Teriyaki Chicken Kabobs 78
Vegetable Garden Fish Kabobs...................86

L

LAMB

Mint Pesto Lamb Chops 38

LEMON

Grilled Lemonade Drummies 25
Lemon Parsley Marinade.............................9
Lemon Zest Dressing Over Fresh Fruit.....104
Sparkling Pink Lemonade.........................124

LIME

Sea Bass With Mango Lime Salsa 67

M

MANGO

Sea Bass With Mango Lime Salsa 67

MARINADE

Balsamic Vinegar & Fresh
Herb Marinade 10
Beef Tenderloin In Sesame Marinade 52
Chicken Breasts Southwestern...................30
Citrus Marinade 8
Coconut Chili Marinade 15
Company's Coming Kabobs........................79
Curry Marinade 12
East Indian Turkey Drumsticks...................19
Fish Steaks With Sweet Red
Pepper Puree 62
Flank Steak In Fajita Marinade 48
Grilled Steaks With Garden Tomato   Basil
Sauce 54
Lemon Parsley Marinade.............................9
Marinated Herb Veal Roast 39
Pork Tenderloin With
Bourbon Marinade 44
Red Wine Marinade 11
Spicy Salsa Verde & Juniper
Berry Marinade.....................................14
Sweet & Tangy Family Steak 46
Teriyaki Chicken Kabobs 78

MUSTARD

Grilled Drumsticks With Zesty Dippers 28
Honey Mustard Glazed Ribs 72
Sweet & Tangy Family Steak 46

O

ONION

Onion Stuffed Hamburgers With
Sloppy Joe Sauce 91
Potato, Cucumber & Onion Salad............116

ORANGE

Glazed Chicken & Orange Salsa.................22

P

PARMESAN

Parmesan Potato & Carrot Bundles 119

PEACH

Swordfish With Peach Pepper Salsa............58

PEANUT/PEANUT BUTTER

Peanut Chicken...24

PECAN

Cheddar Cheese-Pecan Rolled
Flank Steak...50

PEPPERCORN

Pork Chops With Green
Peppercorn Sauce 42

PEPPERS

Fish Steaks With Sweet Red
Pepper Puree 62
Grilled Beef & Pepper Bundles 53
Pineapple Pepper Dip 112
Swordfish With Peach Pepper Salsa............58

PESTO

Mint Pesto Lamb Chops 38

PINEAPPLE

Company's Coming Kabobs........................79
Pineapple Pepper Dip 112
Pineapple-Tarragon Chicken Breasts 35
Teriyaki Chicken Kabobs 78

PIZZA

Mixed Grill Whole Wheat Pizza 97

PORK

Barbecued Pork Sandwiches.....................98
Honey Mustard Glazed Ribs 72
Pork Chops With Green
Peppercorn Sauce.................................42
Pork Roast With Rhubarb Chutney 40
Pork Tenderloin With
Bourbon Marinade 44
Sweet & Tangy Barbecue Sauce With
Country-Style Ribs 73

POTATO

Old-World Potato Salad 118
Parmesan Potato & Carrot Bundles 119
Potato, Cucumber & Onion Salad............116

R

RASPBERRY
Pork Roast With Rhubarb Chutney 40

RELISH
Hamburgers With Cucumber Relish 94

RHUBARB
Pork Roast With Rhubarb Chutney 40

RIBS
Honey Mustard Glazed Ribs 72
Sweet & Tangy Barbecue Sauce With
  Country-Style Ribs 73
Western Barbecued Rib Sampler................74

S

SALAD
Blue Cheese Coleslaw 115
Chicken Vinaigrette Salad 32
Crunchy Cabbage Salad..............................114
Cucumbers In Country Cream 105
Old-World Potato Salad 118
Potato, Cucumber & Onion Salad...........116
Summer Squash Salad 123
Tomato & Cucumber In Vinaigrette 106

SALAD DRESSING
Blue Cheese Coleslaw 115
Chicken Vinaigrette Salad 32
Crunchy Cabbage Salad..............................114

SALMON
Grilled Salmon With Tarragon Butter 64

SALSA
Glazed Chicken & Orange Salsa.................22
Sea Bass With Mango Lime Salsa 67
Spicy Salsa Verde & Juniper
  Berry Marinade 14
Stove Top Spicy Baked Beans....................108
Swordfish With Peach Pepper Salsa...........58

SANDWICH
Barbecued Pork Sandwiches 98
Chutney Grilled Cheese & Ham..............100
Grilled Sausage Patties On Rye 101
Grilled Stuffed Cheeseburger 90
Onion Stuffed Hamburgers With
  Sloppy Joe Sauce 91
Spicy Jumbo Burger Olé 92
Spinach & Swiss Cheese
  Stuffed Hamburgers 96

SAUCE
Apricot Glazed Chicken Breasts.................34
Beef Kabobs With Horseradish Sauce 80
East Indian Turkey Drumsticks 19

Fish Steaks With Sweet   Red
  Pepper Puree 62
Grilled Drumsticks With Zesty Dippers 28
Grilled Garlic Chicken 29
Grilled Steaks With Garden Tomato   Basil
  Sauce 54
Marinated Herb Veal Roast 39
Mixed Grill Whole Wheat Pizza 97
Onion Stuffed Hamburgers With
  Sloppy Joe Sauce 91
Peanut Chicken...24
Pork Chops With Green
  Peppercorn Sauce 42
Spicy Cajun Shrimp 68
Spinach & Swiss Cheese   Stuffed
  Hamburgers.............................96
Sweet & Tangy Barbecue Sauce With
  Country-Style Ribs 73
Swordfish Kabobs 87
Tangy Grilled Chicken 26
Vegetable Garden Fish Kabobs...................86
Western Barbecued Rib Sampler................74

SAUSAGE
Grilled Sausage Patties On Rye 101

SESAME
Beef Tenderloin In Sesame Marinade 52

SHRIMP
Grapefruit & Garlic Shrimp Kabobs...........83
Shrimp Dilled Deviled Eggs.....................111
Spicy Cajun Shrimp 68

SPINACH
Chicken Vinaigrette Salad 32
Grilled Fish Florentine 66
Spinach & Swiss Cheese   Stuffed
  Hamburgers.............................96

SQUASH
Summer Squash Salad 123

STEAK
Cheddar Cheese-Pecan Rolled
  Flank Steak...50
Flank Steak In Fajita Marinade 48
Sweet & Tangy Family Steak 46

STUFFING
Cheddar Cheese-Pecan Rolled
  Flank Steak...50
Grilled Fish Florentine 66

T

TENDERLOIN
Beef Tenderloin In Sesame Marinade 52
Pork Tenderloin With
  Bourbon Marinade 44

TERIYAKI
Teriyaki Chicken Kabobs 78
Vegetable Garden Fish Kabobs...................86

TOMATO
Grilled Steaks With Garden Tomato   Basil
  Sauce 54
Hamburgers With Cucumber Relish 94
Rainbow Trout With Crunchy Gazpacho ...60
Tomato & Cucumber In Vinaigrette 106

TURKEY
East Indian Turkey Drumsticks..................19
Turkey On The Grill...................................20

V

VEAL
Marinated Herb Veal Roast 39

VEGETABLE
Company's Coming Kabobs........................79
Corn On The Cob With
  Seasoned Butters 110
Grilled Garden Kabobs 82
Grilled Garden Vegetables & Sole 59
Parmesan Potato & Carrot Bundles 119
Swordfish Kabobs 87
Teriyaki Chicken Kabobs 78
Vegetable Garden Fish Kabobs...................86

W

WINE
Balsamic Vinegar & Fresh
  Herb Marinade 10
Beef Tenderloin In Sesame Marinade 52
Fish Steaks With Sweet   Red
  Pepper Puree 62
Grapefruit & Garlic Shrimp Kabobs...........83
Red Wine Marinade 11
Spicy Salsa Verde & Juniper   Berry
  Marinade 14

Y

YOGURT
East Indian Turkey Drumsticks..................19

Z

ZUCCHINI
Grilled Garden Vegetables & Sole 59
Summer Squash Salad 123